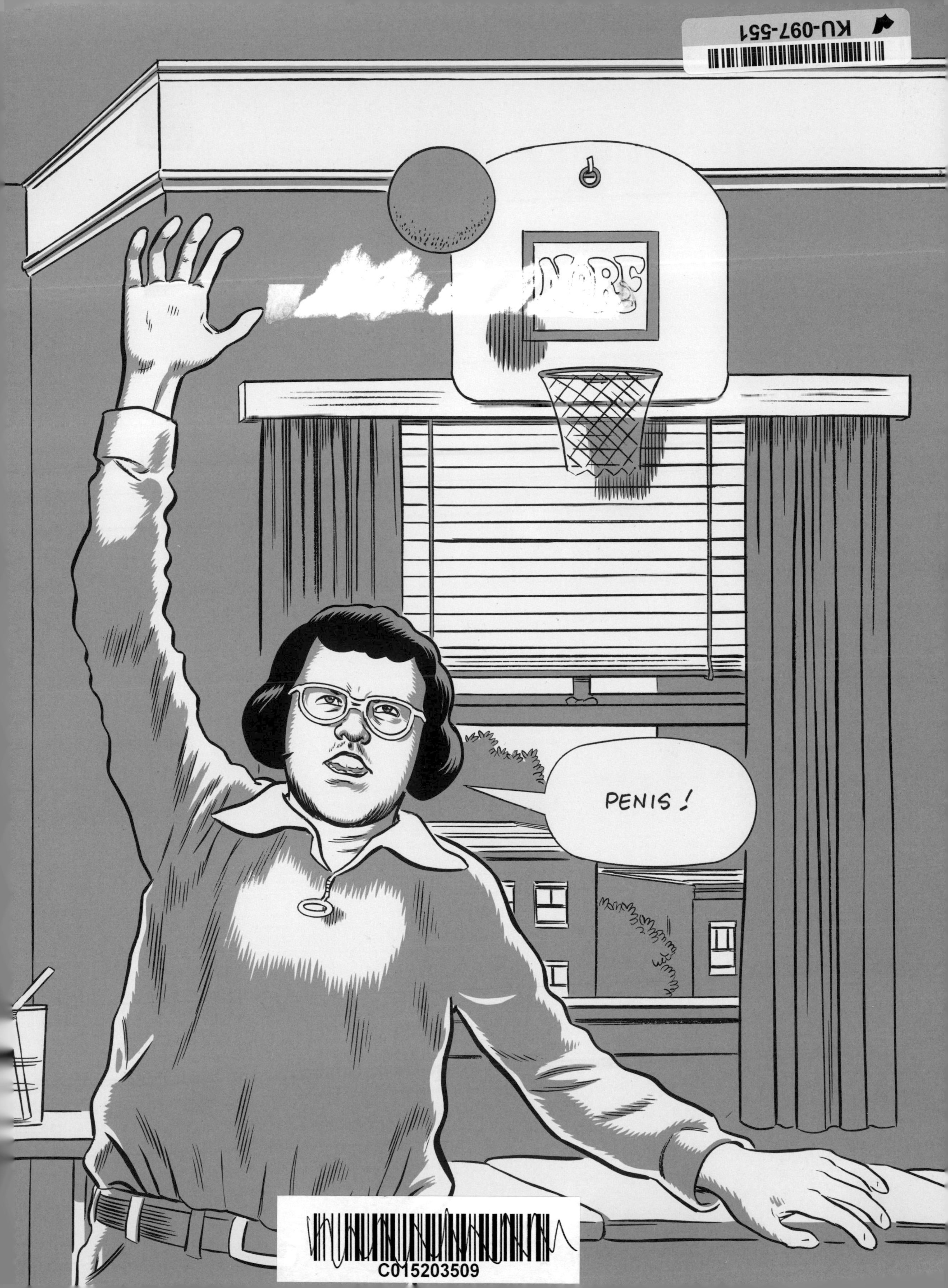
PENIS !

THE DEATH-RAY

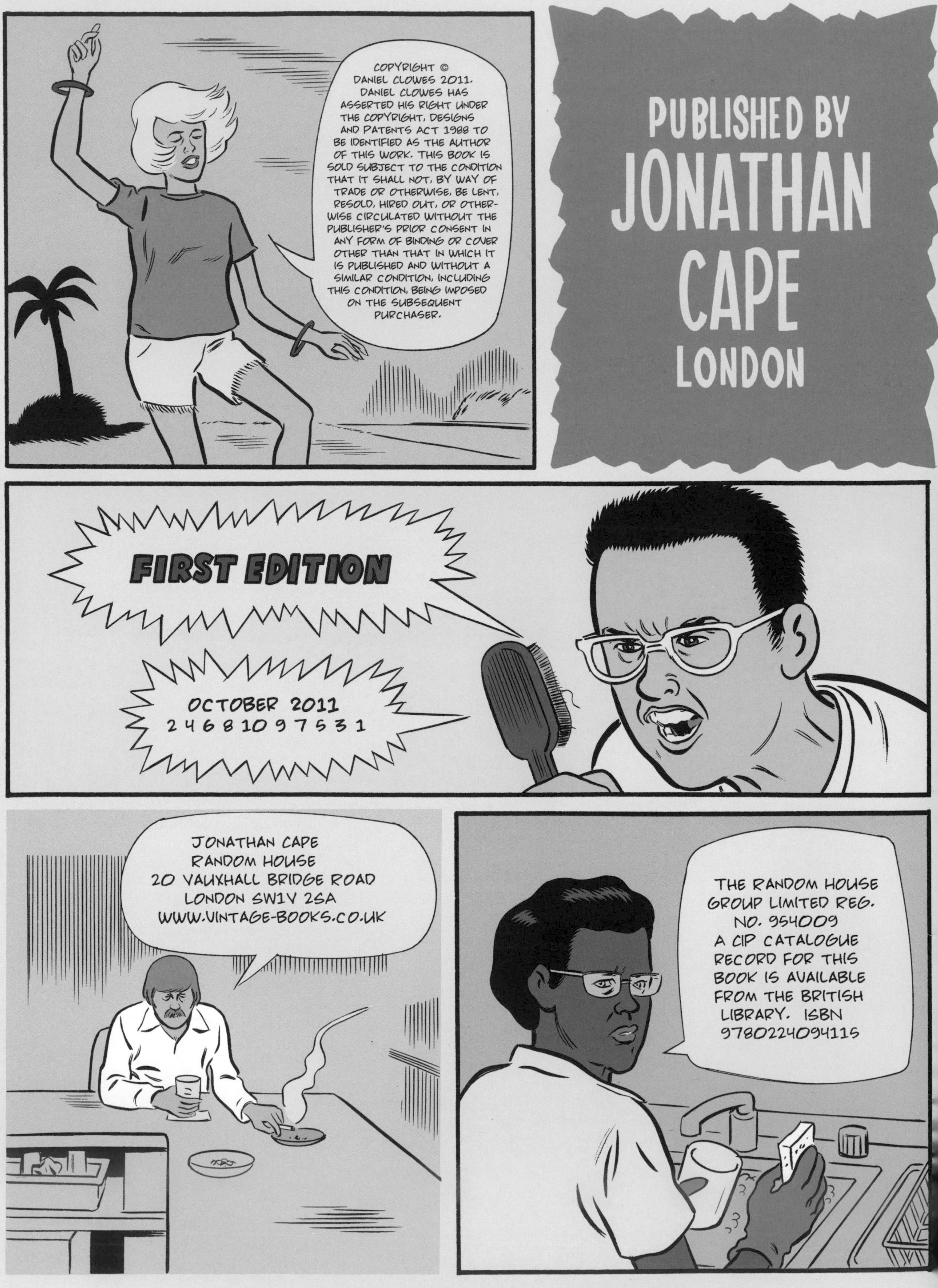
COPYRIGHT © DANIEL CLOWES 2011. DANIEL CLOWES HAS ASSERTED HIS RIGHT UNDER THE COPYRIGHT, DESIGNS AND PATENTS ACT 1988 TO BE IDENTIFIED AS THE AUTHOR OF THIS WORK. THIS BOOK IS SOLD SUBJECT TO THE CONDITION THAT IT SHALL NOT, BY WAY OF TRADE OR OTHERWISE, BE LENT, RESOLD, HIRED OUT, OR OTHERWISE CIRCULATED WITHOUT THE PUBLISHER'S PRIOR CONSENT IN ANY FORM OF BINDING OR COVER OTHER THAN THAT IN WHICH IT IS PUBLISHED AND WITHOUT A SIMILAR CONDITION, INCLUDING THIS CONDITION, BEING IMPOSED ON THE SUBSEQUENT PURCHASER.
PUBLISHED BY JONATHAN CAPE LONDON
FIRST EDITION
OCTOBER 2011
2 4 6 8 10 9 7 5 3 1
JONATHAN CAPE RANDOM HOUSE 20 VAUXHALL BRIDGE ROAD LONDON SW1V 2SA WWW.VINTAGE-BOOKS.CO.UK
THE RANDOM HOUSE GROUP LIMITED REG. NO. 954009 A CIP CATALOGUE RECORD FOR THIS BOOK IS AVAILABLE FROM THE BRITISH LIBRARY. ISBN 9780224094115

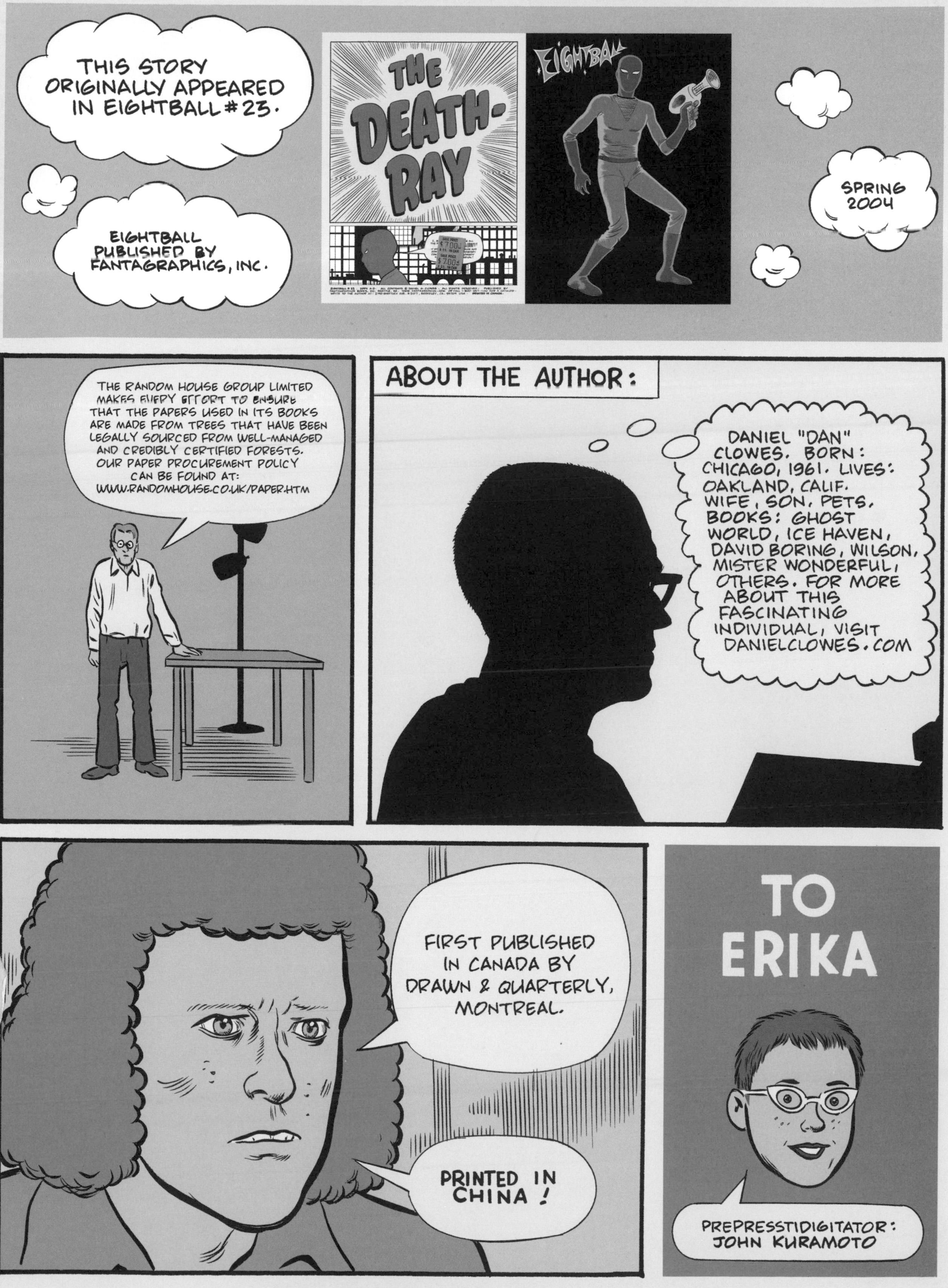
THIS STORY ORIGINALLY APPEARED IN EIGHTBALL #23.
EIGHTBALL PUBLISHED BY FANTAGRAPHICS, INC.
THE DEATH-RAY
EIGHTBALL
SPRING 2004
THE RANDOM HOUSE GROUP LIMITED MAKES EVERY EFFORT TO ENSURE THAT THE PAPERS USED IN ITS BOOKS ARE MADE FROM TREES THAT HAVE BEEN LEGALLY SOURCED FROM WELL-MANAGED AND CREDIBLY CERTIFIED FORESTS. OUR PAPER PROCUREMENT POLICY CAN BE FOUND AT: WWW.RANDOMHOUSE.CO.UK/PAPER.HTM
ABOUT THE AUTHOR:
DANIEL "DAN" CLOWES. BORN: CHICAGO, 1961. LIVES: OAKLAND, CALIF. WIFE, SON, PETS. BOOKS: GHOST WORLD, ICE HAVEN, DAVID BORING, WILSON, MISTER WONDERFUL, OTHERS. FOR MORE ABOUT THIS FASCINATING INDIVIDUAL, VISIT DANIELCLOWES.COM
FIRST PUBLISHED IN CANADA BY DRAWN & QUARTERLY, MONTREAL.
PRINTED IN CHINA!
TO ERIKA
PREPRESSTIDIGITATOR: JOHN KURAMOTO

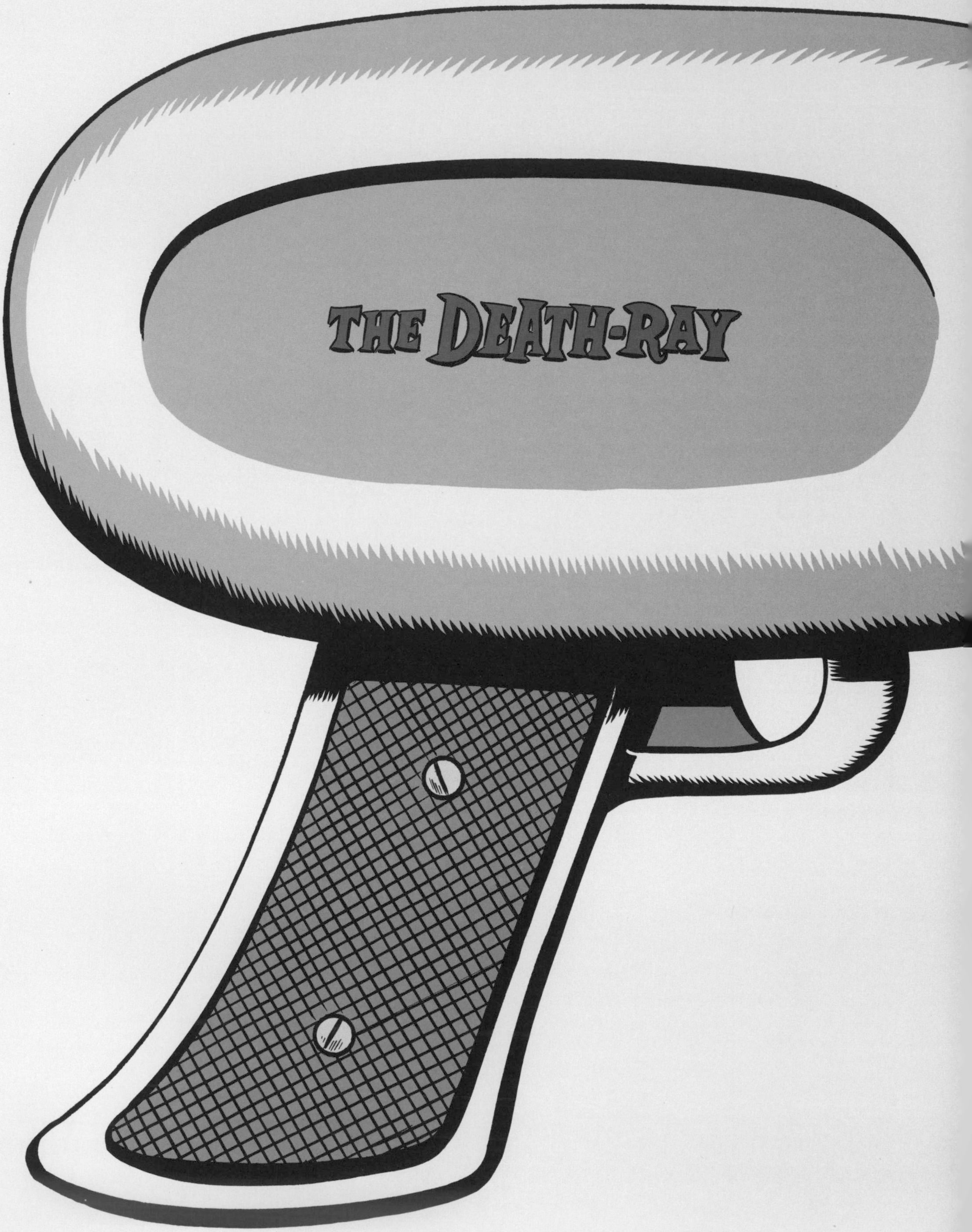
THE DEATH-RAY

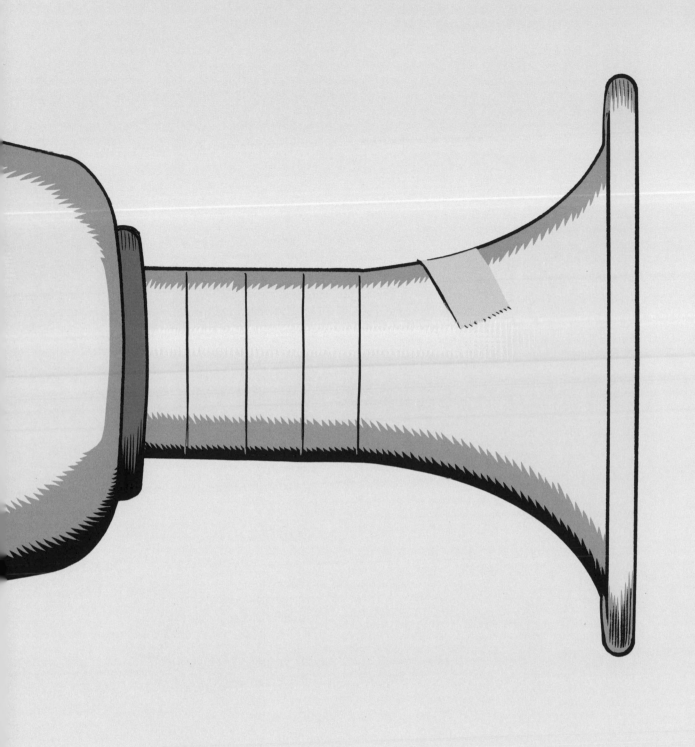

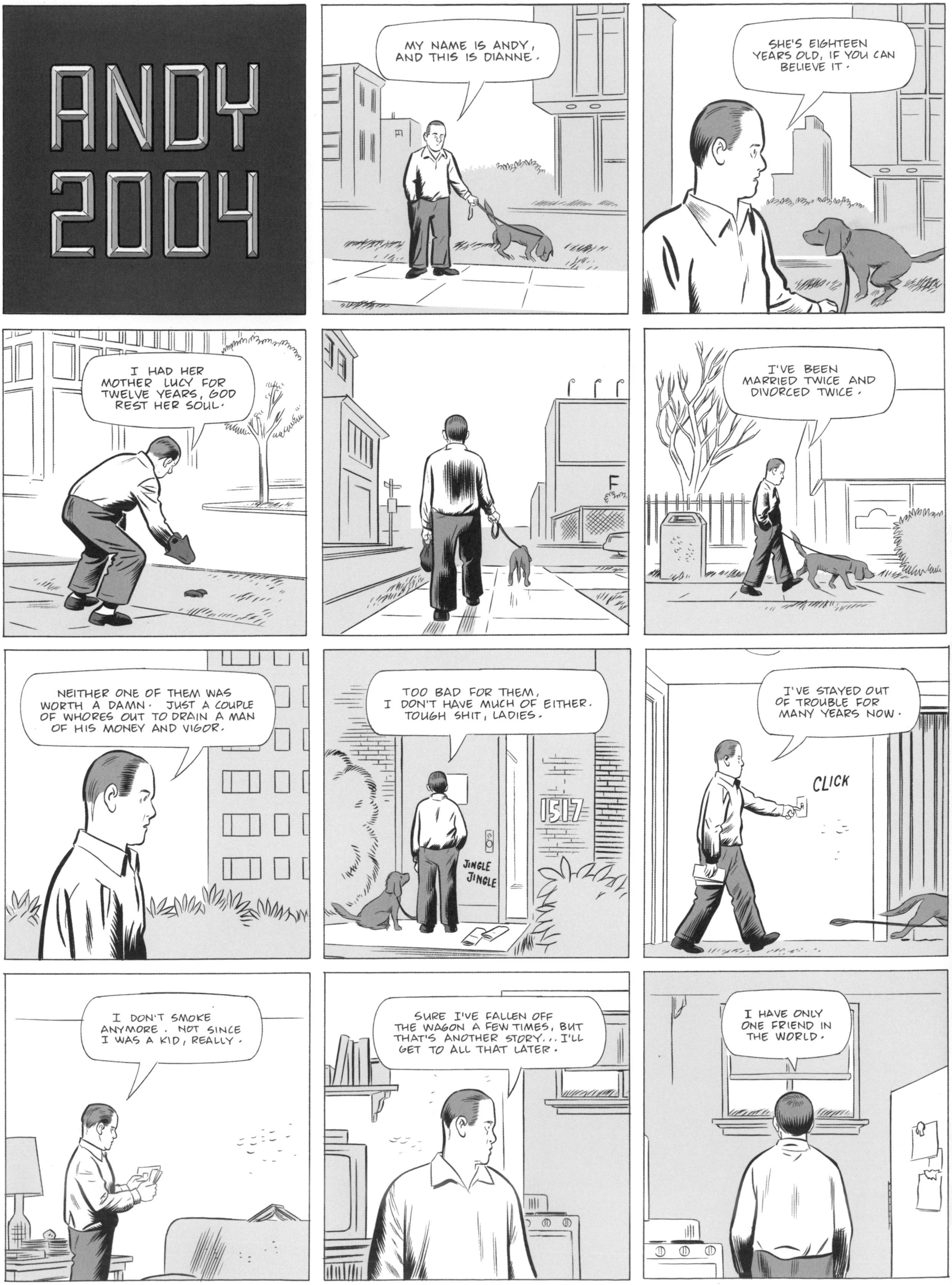
ANDY 2004
MY NAME IS ANDY, AND THIS IS DIANNE.
SHE'S EIGHTEEN YEARS OLD, IF YOU CAN BELIEVE IT.
I HAD HER MOTHER LUCY FOR TWELVE YEARS, GOD REST HER SOUL.
F
I'VE BEEN MARRIED TWICE AND DIVORCED TWICE.
NEITHER ONE OF THEM WAS WORTH A DAMN. JUST A COUPLE OF WHORES OUT TO DRAIN A MAN OF HIS MONEY AND VIGOR.
TOO BAD FOR THEM, I DON'T HAVE MUCH OF EITHER. TOUGH SHIT, LADIES.
1517
JINGLE JINGLE
I'VE STAYED OUT OF TROUBLE FOR MANY YEARS NOW.
CLICK
I DON'T SMOKE ANYMORE. NOT SINCE I WAS A KID, REALLY.
SURE I'VE FALLEN OFF THE WAGON A FEW TIMES, BUT THAT'S ANOTHER STORY... I'LL GET TO ALL THAT LATER.
I HAVE ONLY ONE FRIEND IN THE WORLD.

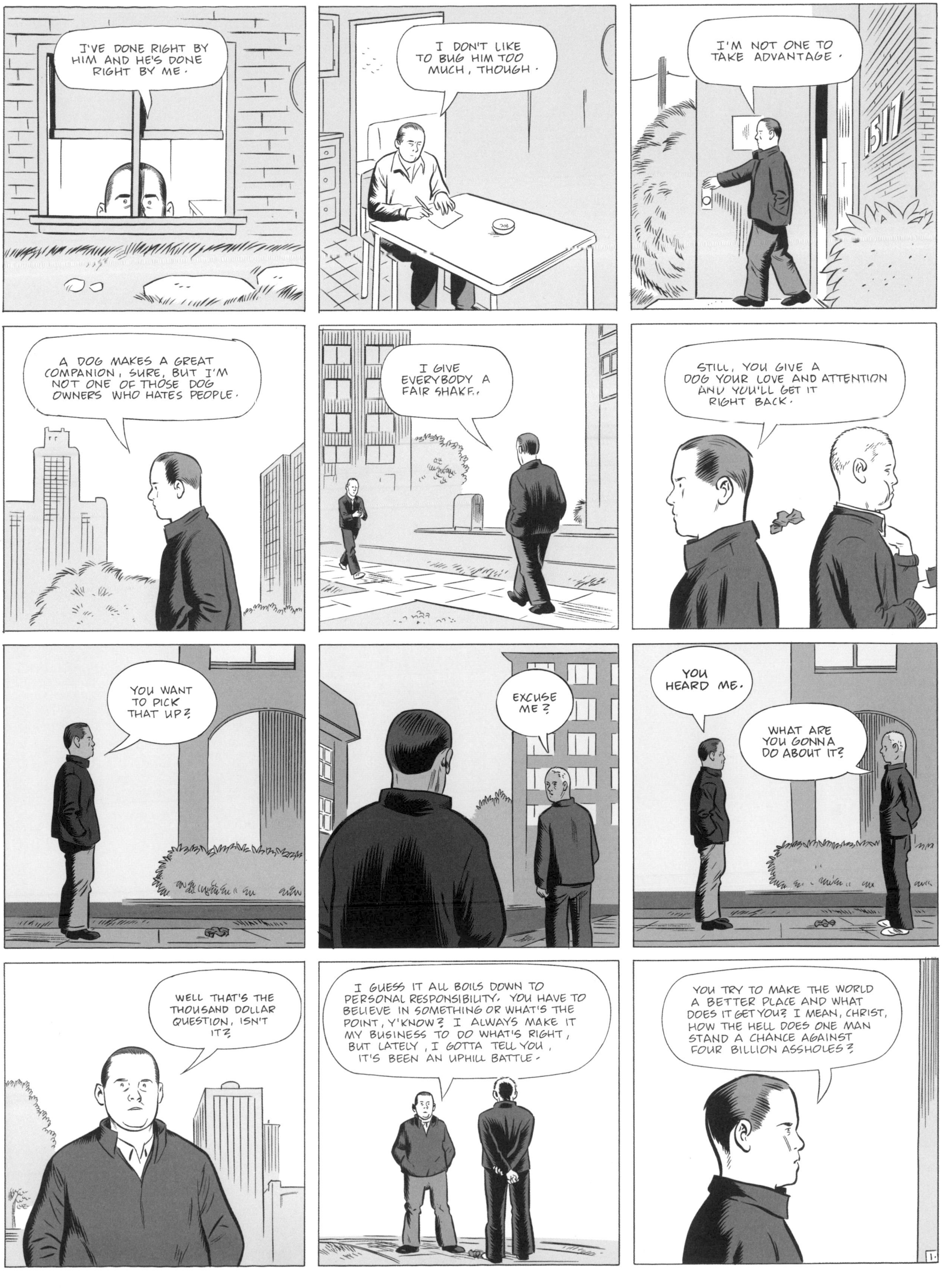

I'VE DONE RIGHT BY HIM AND HE'S DONE RIGHT BY ME.
I DON'T LIKE TO BUG HIM TOO MUCH, THOUGH.
I'M NOT ONE TO TAKE ADVANTAGE.
1517
A DOG MAKES A GREAT COMPANION, SURE, BUT I'M NOT ONE OF THOSE DOG OWNERS WHO HATES PEOPLE.
I GIVE EVERYBODY A FAIR SHAKE.
STILL, YOU GIVE A DOG YOUR LOVE AND ATTENTION AND YOU'LL GET IT RIGHT BACK.
YOU WANT TO PICK THAT UP?
EXCUSE ME?
YOU HEARD ME.
WHAT ARE YOU GONNA DO ABOUT IT?
WELL THAT'S THE THOUSAND DOLLAR QUESTION, ISN'T IT?
I GUESS IT ALL BOILS DOWN TO PERSONAL RESPONSIBILITY. YOU HAVE TO BELIEVE IN SOMETHING OR WHAT'S THE POINT, Y'KNOW? I ALWAYS MAKE IT MY BUSINESS TO DO WHAT'S RIGHT, BUT LATELY, I GOTTA TELL YOU, IT'S BEEN AN UPHILL BATTLE.
YOU TRY TO MAKE THE WORLD A BETTER PLACE AND WHAT DOES IT GET YOU? I MEAN, CHRIST, HOW THE HELL DOES ONE MAN STAND A CHANCE AGAINST FOUR BILLION ASSHOLES?

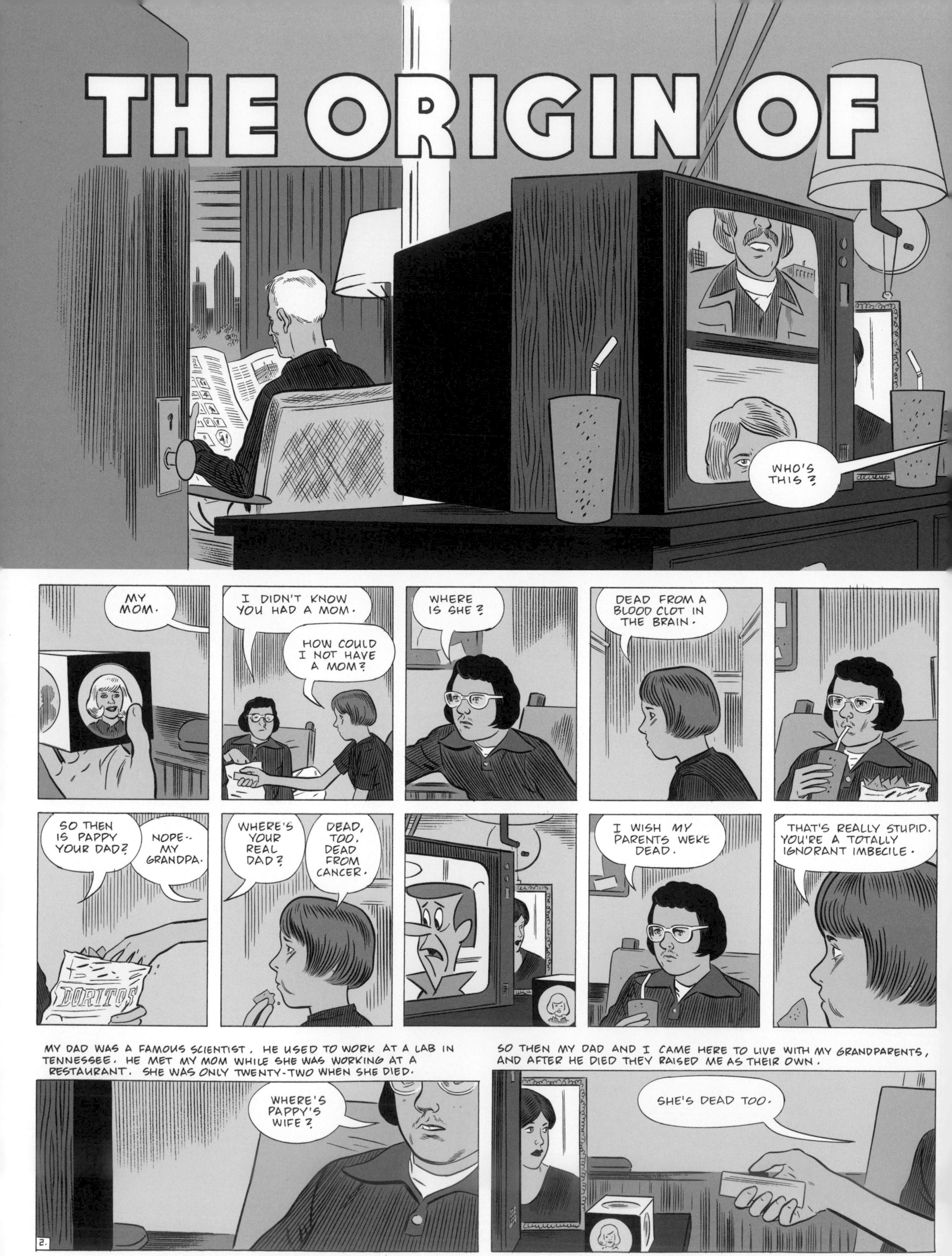
THE ORIGIN OF
WHO'S THIS?
MY MOM.
I DIDN'T KNOW YOU HAD A MOM.
HOW COULD I NOT HAVE A MOM?
WHERE IS SHE?
DEAD FROM A BLOOD CLOT IN THE BRAIN.
SO THEN IS PAPPY YOUR DAD?
NOPE-- MY GRANDPA.
WHERE'S YOUR REAL DAD?
DEAD, TOO. DEAD FROM CANCER.
I WISH MY PARENTS WERE DEAD.
THAT'S REALLY STUPID. YOU'RE A TOTALLY IGNORANT IMBECILE.
DORITOS
MY DAD WAS A FAMOUS SCIENTIST. HE USED TO WORK AT A LAB IN TENNESSEE. HE MET MY MOM WHILE SHE WAS WORKING AT A RESTAURANT. SHE WAS ONLY TWENTY-TWO WHEN SHE DIED.
WHERE'S PAPPY'S WIFE?
SO THEN MY DAD AND I CAME HERE TO LIVE WITH MY GRANDPARENTS, AND AFTER HE DIED THEY RAISED ME AS THEIR OWN.
SHE'S DEAD TOO.

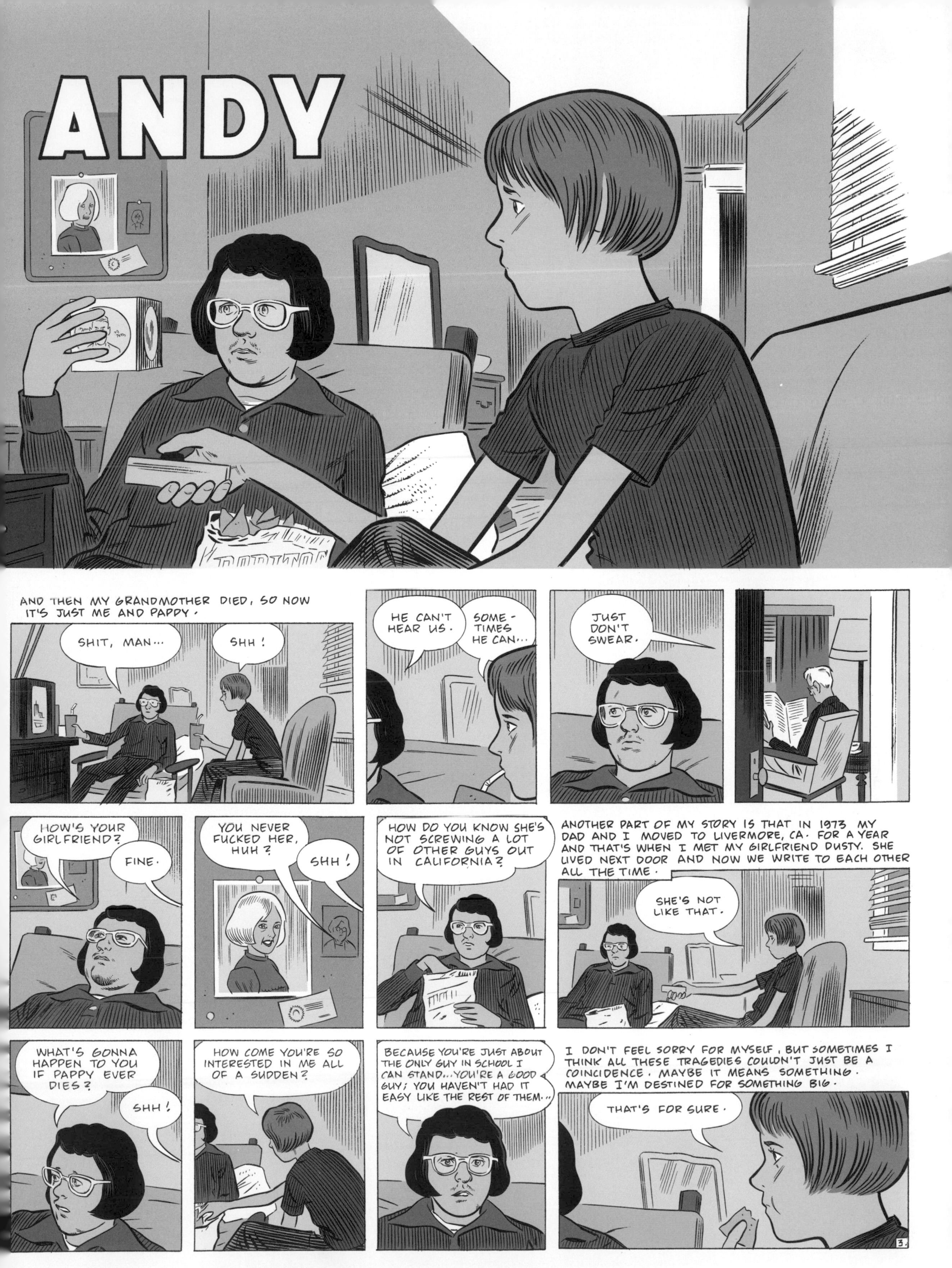
ANDY
DORITOS
AND THEN MY GRANDMOTHER DIED, SO NOW IT'S JUST ME AND PAPPY.
SHIT, MAN...
SHH!
HE CAN'T HEAR US.
SOME-TIMES HE CAN...
JUST DON'T SWEAR.
HOW'S YOUR GIRLFRIEND?
FINE.
YOU NEVER FUCKED HER, HUH?
SHH!
HOW DO YOU KNOW SHE'S NOT SCREWING A LOT OF OTHER GUYS OUT IN CALIFORNIA?
ANOTHER PART OF MY STORY IS THAT IN 1973 MY DAD AND I MOVED TO LIVERMORE, CA. FOR A YEAR AND THAT'S WHEN I MET MY GIRLFRIEND DUSTY. SHE LIVED NEXT DOOR AND NOW WE WRITE TO EACH OTHER ALL THE TIME.
SHE'S NOT LIKE THAT.
WHAT'S GONNA HAPPEN TO YOU IF PAPPY EVER DIES?
SHH!
HOW COME YOU'RE SO INTERESTED IN ME ALL OF A SUDDEN?
BECAUSE YOU'RE JUST ABOUT THE ONLY GUY IN SCHOOL I CAN STAND... YOU'RE A GOOD GUY; YOU HAVEN'T HAD IT EASY LIKE THE REST OF THEM...
I DON'T FEEL SORRY FOR MYSELF, BUT SOMETIMES I THINK ALL THESE TRAGEDIES COULDN'T JUST BE A COINCIDENCE. MAYBE IT MEANS SOMETHING. MAYBE I'M DESTINED FOR SOMETHING BIG.
THAT'S FOR SURE.
3.

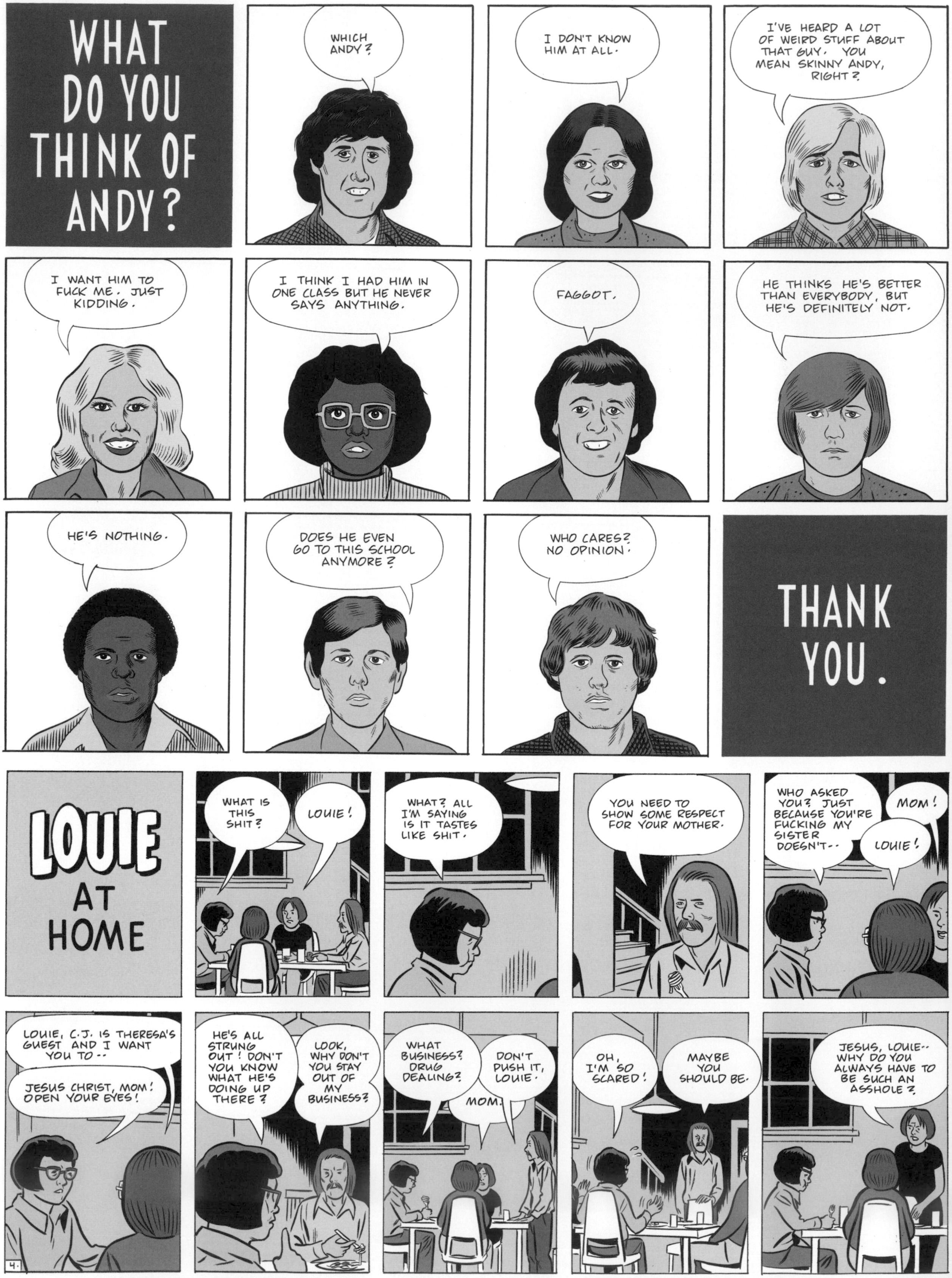
WHAT DO YOU THINK OF ANDY?
WHICH ANDY?
I DON'T KNOW HIM AT ALL.
I'VE HEARD A LOT OF WEIRD STUFF ABOUT THAT GUY. YOU MEAN SKINNY ANDY, RIGHT?
I WANT HIM TO FUCK ME. JUST KIDDING.
I THINK I HAD HIM IN ONE CLASS BUT HE NEVER SAYS ANYTHING.
FAGGOT.
HE THINKS HE'S BETTER THAN EVERYBODY, BUT HE'S DEFINITELY NOT.
HE'S NOTHING.
DOES HE EVEN GO TO THIS SCHOOL ANYMORE?
WHO CARES? NO OPINION.
THANK YOU.
LOUIE AT HOME
WHAT IS THIS SHIT?
LOUIE!
WHAT? ALL I'M SAYING IS IT TASTES LIKE SHIT.
YOU NEED TO SHOW SOME RESPECT FOR YOUR MOTHER.
WHO ASKED YOU? JUST BECAUSE YOU'RE FUCKING MY SISTER DOESN'T--
MOM!
LOUIE!
LOUIE, C.J. IS THERESA'S GUEST AND I WANT YOU TO--
JESUS CHRIST, MOM! OPEN YOUR EYES!
HE'S ALL STRUNG OUT! DON'T YOU KNOW WHAT HE'S DOING UP THERE?
LOOK, WHY DON'T YOU STAY OUT OF MY BUSINESS?
WHAT BUSINESS? DRUG DEALING?
DON'T PUSH IT, LOUIE.
MOM.
OH, I'M SO SCARED!
MAYBE YOU SHOULD BE.
JESUS, LOUIE-- WHY DO YOU ALWAYS HAVE TO BE SUCH AN ASSHOLE?

ANDY'S WORLD

5.

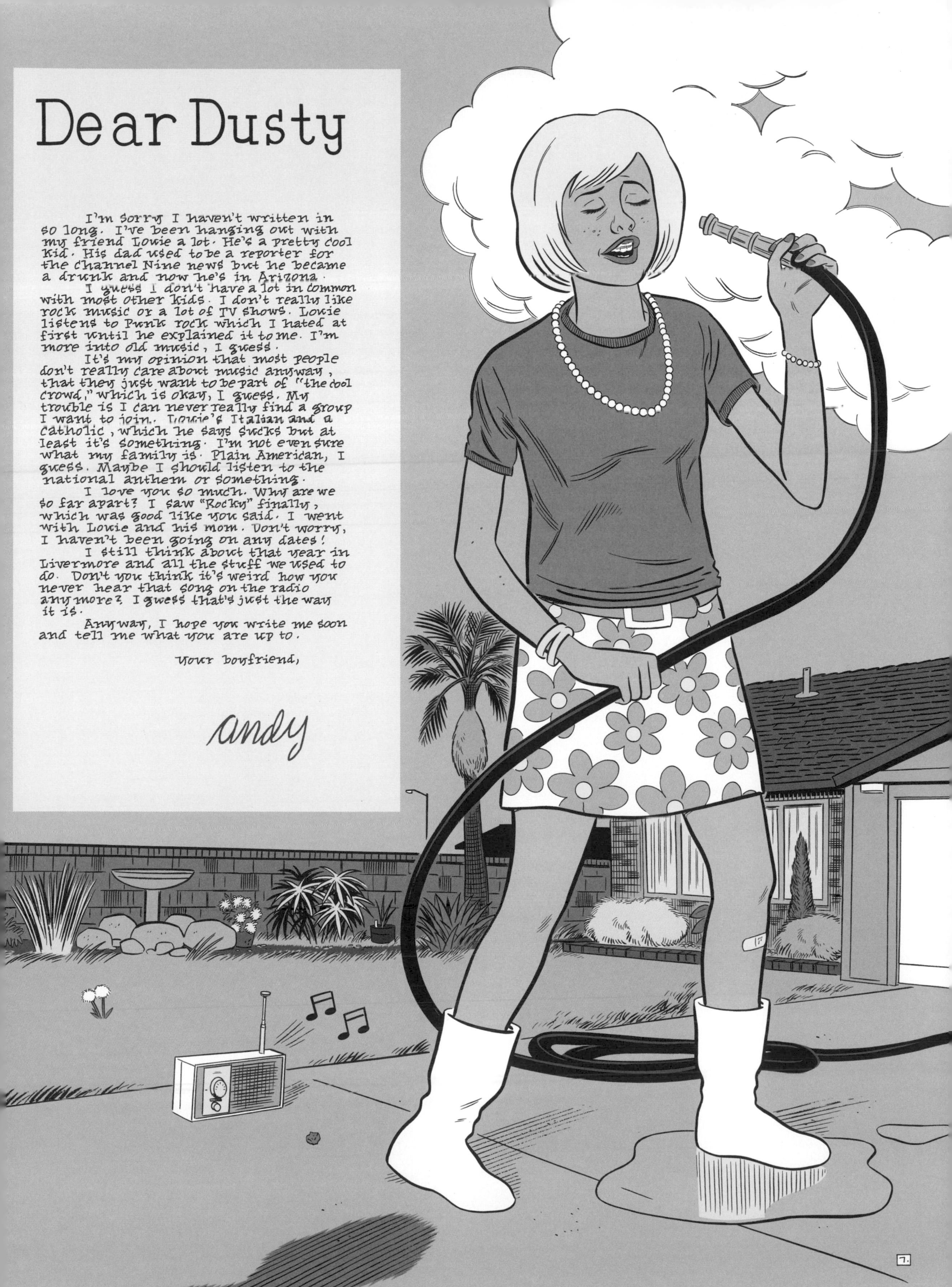
Dear Dusty
I'm sorry I haven't written in so long. I've been hanging out with my friend Louie a lot. He's a pretty cool kid. His dad used to be a reporter for the Channel Nine news but he became a drunk and now he's in Arizona.
I guess I don't have a lot in common with most other kids. I don't really like rock music or a lot of TV shows. Louie listens to Punk rock which I hated at first until he explained it to me. I'm more into old music, I guess.
It's my opinion that most people don't really care about music anyway, that they just want to be part of "the cool crowd," which is okay, I guess. My trouble is I can never really find a group I want to join. Louie's Italian and a Catholic, which he says sucks but at least it's something. I'm not even sure what my family is. Plain American, I guess. Maybe I should listen to the national anthem or something.
I love you so much. Why are we so far apart? I saw "Rocky" finally, which was good like you said. I went with Louie and his mom. Don't worry, I haven't been going on any dates!
I still think about that year in Livermore and all the stuff we used to do. Don't you think it's weird how you never hear that song on the radio anymore? I guess that's just the way it is.
Anyway, I hope you write me soon and tell me what you are up to.
Your boyfriend,
andy

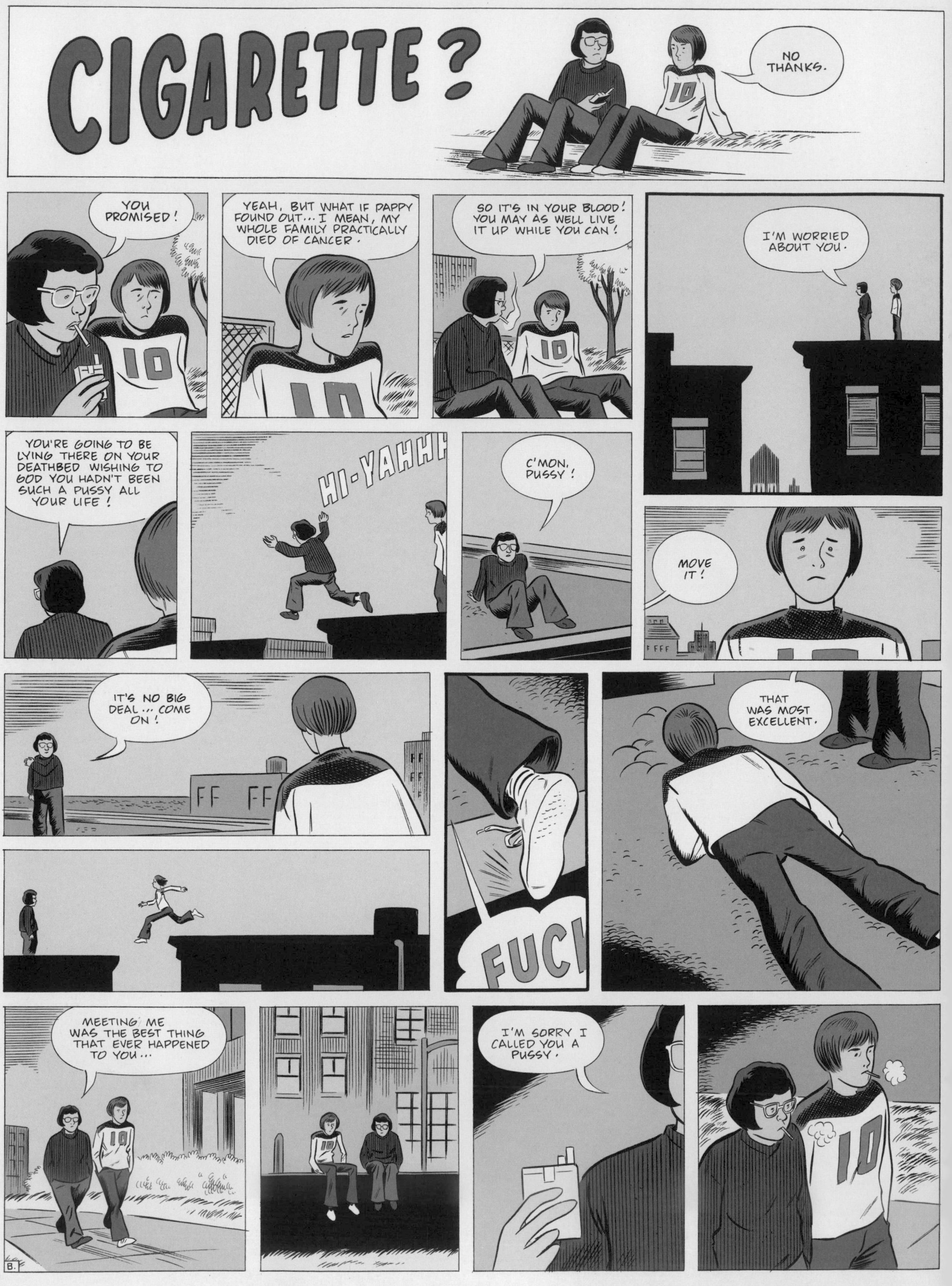
CIGARETTE?
NO THANKS.
YOU PROMISED!
YEAH, BUT WHAT IF PAPPY FOUND OUT... I MEAN, MY WHOLE FAMILY PRACTICALLY DIED OF CANCER.
SO IT'S IN YOUR BLOOD! YOU MAY AS WELL LIVE IT UP WHILE YOU CAN!
I'M WORRIED ABOUT YOU.
YOU'RE GOING TO BE LYING THERE ON YOUR DEATHBED WISHING TO GOD YOU HADN'T BEEN SUCH A PUSSY ALL YOUR LIFE!
HI-YAHHH
C'MON, PUSSY!
MOVE IT!
IT'S NO BIG DEAL... COME ON!
FUC
THAT WAS MOST EXCELLENT.
MEETING ME WAS THE BEST THING THAT EVER HAPPENED TO YOU...
I'M SORRY I CALLED YOU A PUSSY.
B.

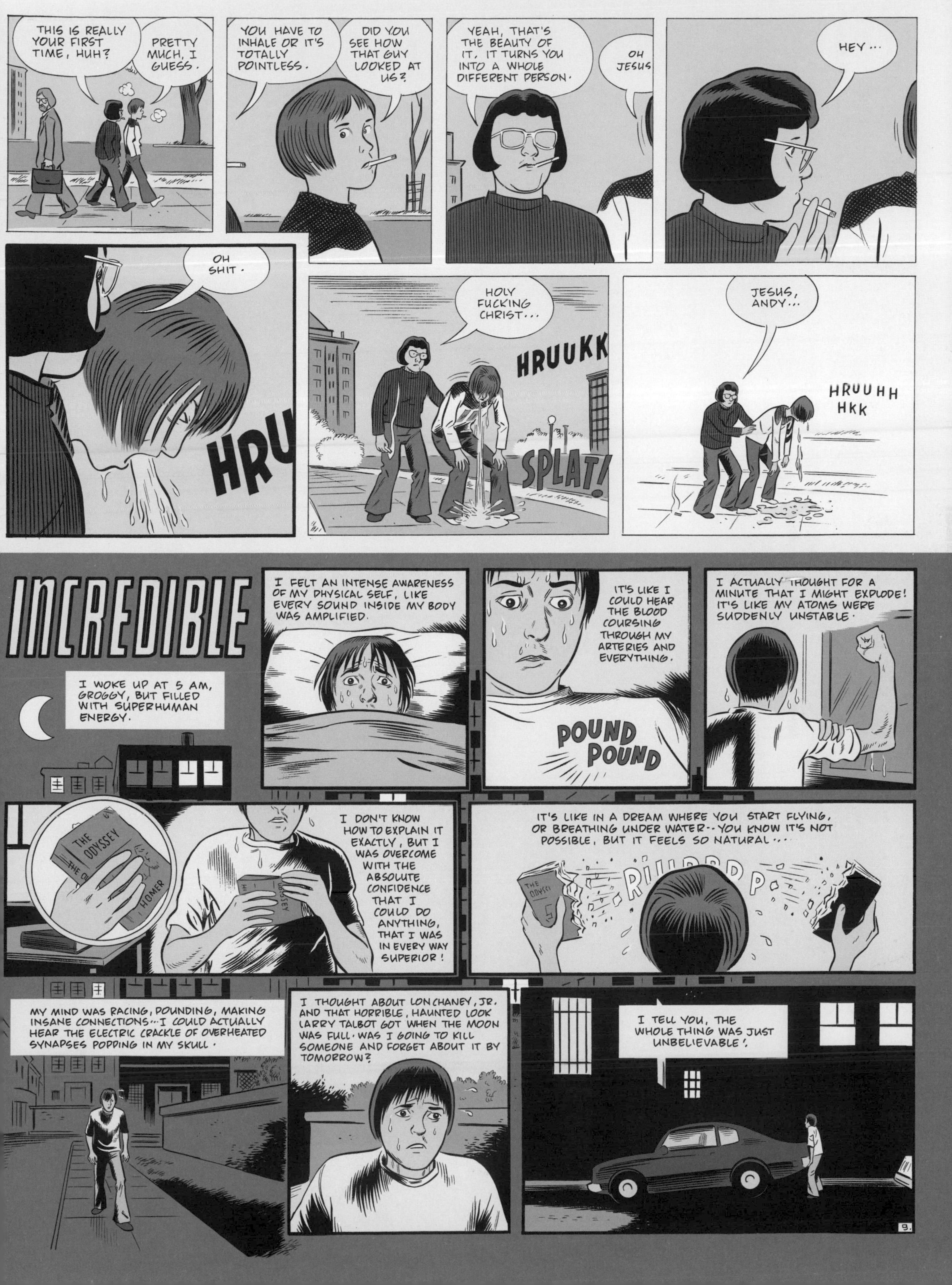
THIS IS REALLY YOUR FIRST TIME, HUH?
PRETTY MUCH, I GUESS.
YOU HAVE TO INHALE OR IT'S TOTALLY POINTLESS.
DID YOU SEE HOW THAT GUY LOOKED AT US?
YEAH, THAT'S THE BEAUTY OF IT, IT TURNS YOU INTO A WHOLE DIFFERENT PERSON.
OH JESUS
HEY...
OH SHIT.
HRU
HOLY FUCKING CHRIST...
HRUUKK
SPLAT!
JESUS, ANDY...
HRUUHH HKK
INCREDIBLE
I WOKE UP AT 5 AM, GROGGY, BUT FILLED WITH SUPERHUMAN ENERGY.
I FELT AN INTENSE AWARENESS OF MY PHYSICAL SELF, LIKE EVERY SOUND INSIDE MY BODY WAS AMPLIFIED.
IT'S LIKE I COULD HEAR THE BLOOD COURSING THROUGH MY ARTERIES AND EVERYTHING.
POUND POUND
I ACTUALLY THOUGHT FOR A MINUTE THAT I MIGHT EXPLODE! IT'S LIKE MY ATOMS WERE SUDDENLY UNSTABLE.
THE ODYSSEY
HOMER
I DON'T KNOW HOW TO EXPLAIN IT EXACTLY, BUT I WAS OVERCOME WITH THE ABSOLUTE CONFIDENCE THAT I COULD DO ANYTHING, THAT I WAS IN EVERY WAY SUPERIOR!
IT'S LIKE IN A DREAM WHERE YOU START FLYING, OR BREATHING UNDER WATER.. YOU KNOW IT'S NOT POSSIBLE, BUT IT FEELS SO NATURAL...
RIIIPPPP
MY MIND WAS RACING, POUNDING, MAKING INSANE CONNECTIONS... I COULD ACTUALLY HEAR THE ELECTRIC CRACKLE OF OVERHEATED SYNAPSES POPPING IN MY SKULL.
I THOUGHT ABOUT LON CHANEY, JR. AND THAT HORRIBLE, HAUNTED LOOK LARRY TALBOT GOT WHEN THE MOON WAS FULL. WAS I GOING TO KILL SOMEONE AND FORGET ABOUT IT BY TOMORROW?
I TELL YOU, THE WHOLE THING WAS JUST UNBELIEVABLE!
9.

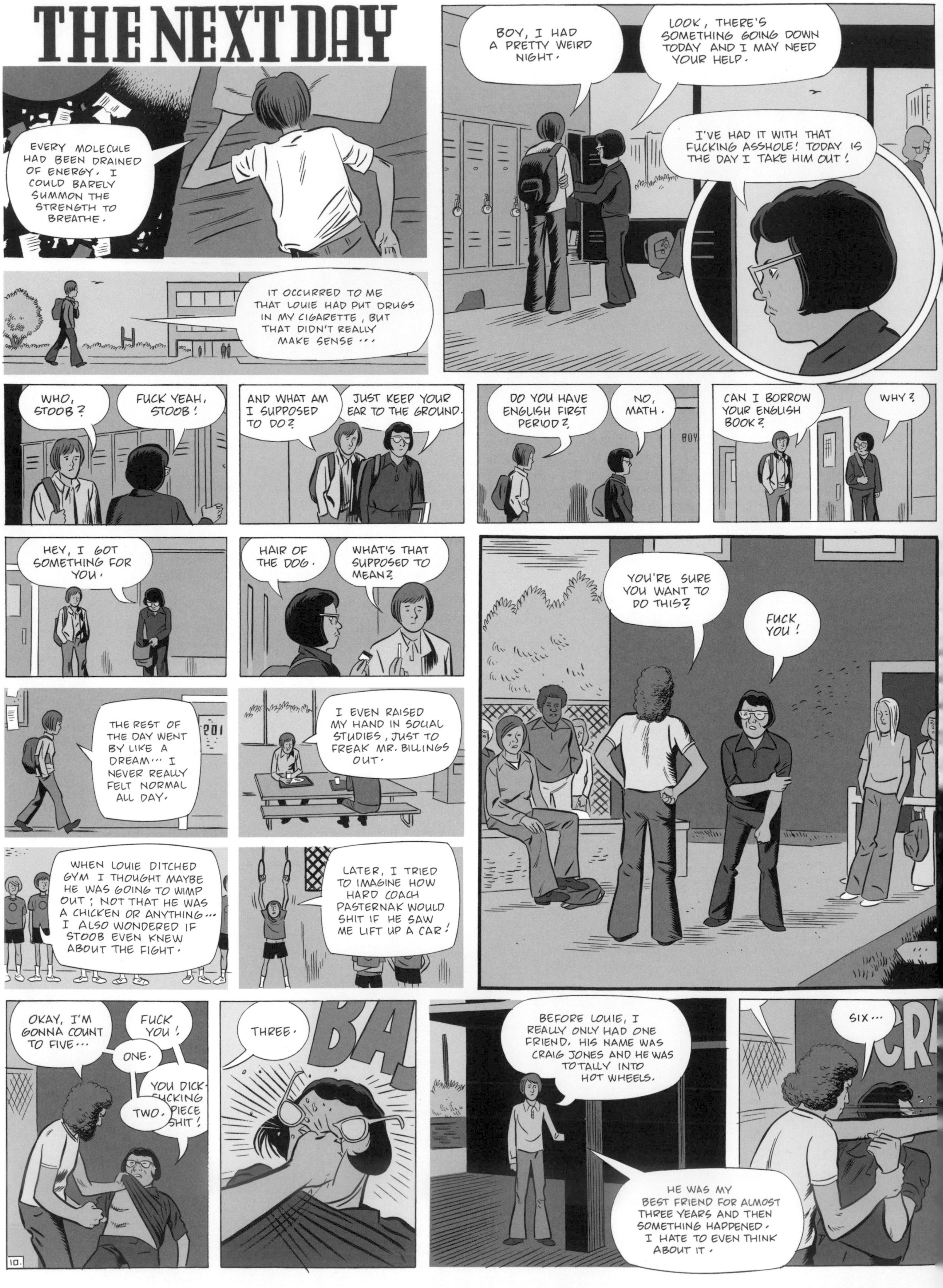

THE NEXT DAY
EVERY MOLECULE HAD BEEN DRAINED OF ENERGY. I COULD BARELY SUMMON THE STRENGTH TO BREATHE.
IT OCCURRED TO ME THAT LOUIE HAD PUT DRUGS IN MY CIGARETTE, BUT THAT DIDN'T REALLY MAKE SENSE...
BOY, I HAD A PRETTY WEIRD NIGHT.
LOOK, THERE'S SOMETHING GOING DOWN TODAY AND I MAY NEED YOUR HELP.
I'VE HAD IT WITH THAT FUCKING ASSHOLE! TODAY IS THE DAY I TAKE HIM OUT!
WHO, STOOB?
FUCK YEAH, STOOB!
AND WHAT AM I SUPPOSED TO DO?
JUST KEEP YOUR EAR TO THE GROUND.
DO YOU HAVE ENGLISH FIRST PERIOD?
NO, MATH.
BOY
CAN I BORROW YOUR ENGLISH BOOK?
WHY?
HEY, I GOT SOMETHING FOR YOU.
HAIR OF THE DOG.
WHAT'S THAT SUPPOSED TO MEAN?
THE REST OF THE DAY WENT BY LIKE A DREAM... I NEVER REALLY FELT NORMAL ALL DAY.
201
I EVEN RAISED MY HAND IN SOCIAL STUDIES, JUST TO FREAK MR. BILLINGS OUT.
WHEN LOUIE DITCHED GYM I THOUGHT MAYBE HE WAS GOING TO WIMP OUT; NOT THAT HE WAS A CHICKEN OR ANYTHING... I ALSO WONDERED IF STOOB EVEN KNEW ABOUT THE FIGHT.
LATER, I TRIED TO IMAGINE HOW HARD COACH PASTERNAK WOULD SHIT IF HE SAW ME LIFT UP A CAR!
YOU'RE SURE YOU WANT TO DO THIS?
FUCK YOU!
OKAY, I'M GONNA COUNT TO FIVE...
FUCK YOU!
ONE.
YOU DICK-SUCKING PIECE SHIT!
TWO.
THREE.
BA
BEFORE LOUIE, I REALLY ONLY HAD ONE FRIEND. HIS NAME WAS CRAIG JONES AND HE WAS TOTALLY INTO HOT WHEELS.
HE WAS MY BEST FRIEND FOR ALMOST THREE YEARS AND THEN SOMETHING HAPPENED. I HATE TO EVEN THINK ABOUT IT.
SIX...
CR

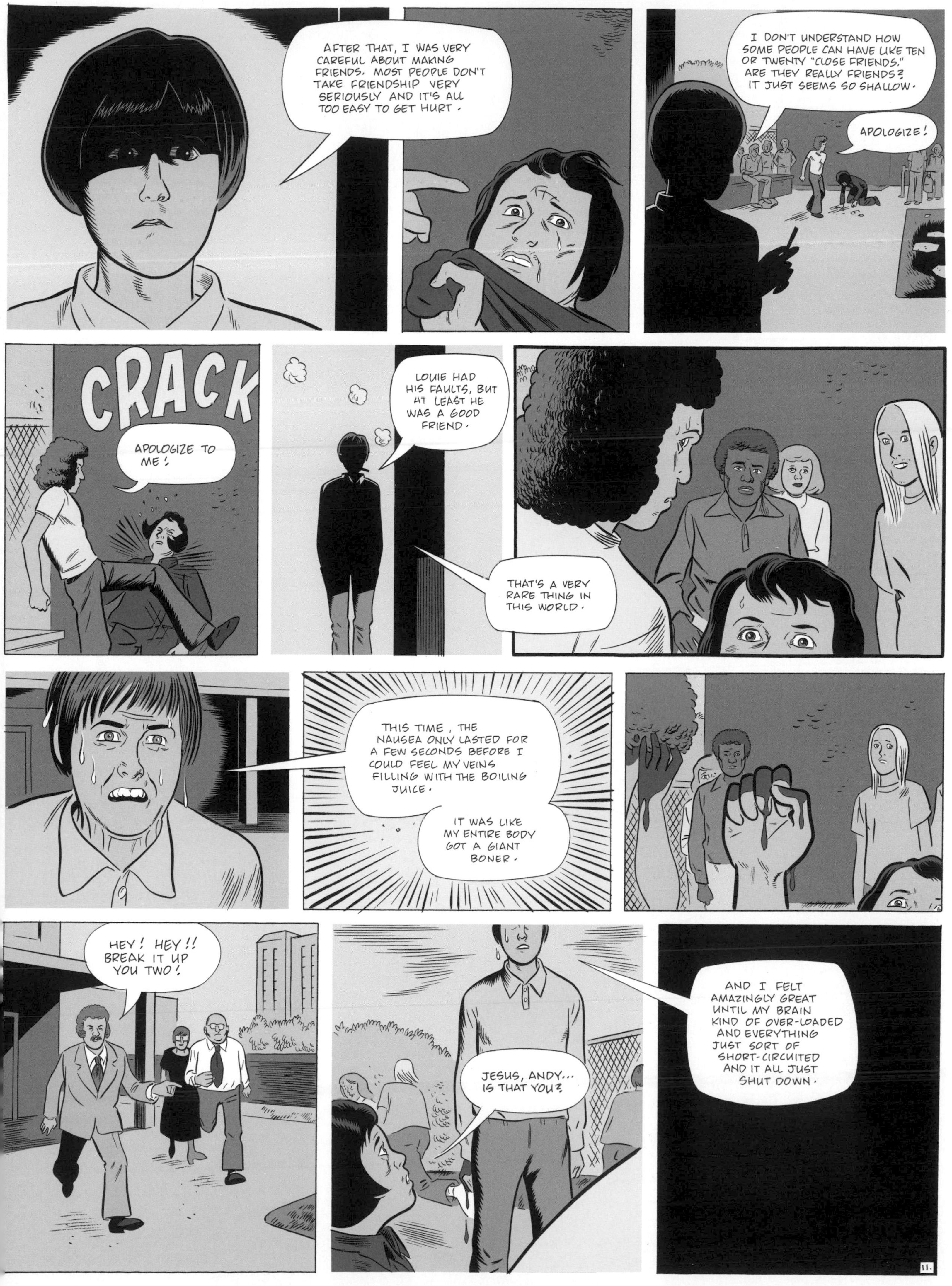

AFTER THAT, I WAS VERY CAREFUL ABOUT MAKING FRIENDS. MOST PEOPLE DON'T TAKE FRIENDSHIP VERY SERIOUSLY AND IT'S ALL TOO EASY TO GET HURT.
I DON'T UNDERSTAND HOW SOME PEOPLE CAN HAVE LIKE TEN OR TWENTY "CLOSE FRIENDS." ARE THEY REALLY FRIENDS? IT JUST SEEMS SO SHALLOW.
APOLOGIZE!
CRACK
APOLOGIZE TO ME!
LOUIE HAD HIS FAULTS, BUT AT LEAST HE WAS A GOOD FRIEND.
THAT'S A VERY RARE THING IN THIS WORLD.
THIS TIME, THE NAUSEA ONLY LASTED FOR A FEW SECONDS BEFORE I COULD FEEL MY VEINS FILLING WITH THE BOILING JUICE.
IT WAS LIKE MY ENTIRE BODY GOT A GIANT BONER.
HEY! HEY!! BREAK IT UP YOU TWO!
JESUS, ANDY... IS THAT YOU?
AND I FELT AMAZINGLY GREAT UNTIL MY BRAIN KIND OF OVER-LOADED AND EVERYTHING JUST SORT OF SHORT-CIRCUITED AND IT ALL JUST SHUT DOWN.

FUCK ME, ANDY!

THE

YEAH, BABY—— THAT'S IT!

SO HERE'S WHAT HAPPENED: I GOT A TERRIBLE HEADACHE AND MISSED THE NEXT TWO WEEK'S OF SCHOOL, AND THEN IT WAS SPRING VACATION. LOUIE WENT TO NEW YORK TO VISIT HIS LEZZIE SISTER AND SO I SPENT THE WHOLE TIME PRETTY MUCH ALONE.

DURING THE WEEK OFF I STARTED TO EXPERIMENT WITH THE CIGARETTES, TAKING A FEW LITTLE PUFFS AT A TIME. I GOT SO I COULD MAINTAIN A LOW LEVEL OF THE ENERGY WITHOUT GETTING MUCH OF A HEADACHE AT ALL.

TINK

ORIGIN

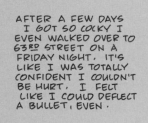

AFTER A FEW DAYS I GOT SO COCKY I EVEN WALKED OVER TO 63RD STREET ON A FRIDAY NIGHT. IT'S LIKE I WAS TOTALLY CONFIDENT I COULDN'T BE HURT. I FELT LIKE I COULD DEFLECT A BULLET, EVEN.

SAY, BOY....

YOU GOT ANOTHER CIGARETTE, BOY?

ANDY?

LORD A'MIGHTY, ANDY, ARE YOU CRAZY?! YOU CAN'T BE WALKING OVER HERE AT NIGHT!

I SAW WHAT YOU DID! WHY ARE YOU ACTING UP ON ME, ANDY?

YOU ALWAYS BEEN A GOOD BOY, ANDY—— WHAT HAPPENED TO YOU?

I SWEAR YOU'RE GONNA PUT YOUR GRANDPAPPY IN AN EARLY GRAVE!

OH ANDY, YOU FUCK ME SO GOOD!

OF

I'M IN BIG TROUBLE...

I'LL TELL YOU LATER.. I CAN'T TALK...

WHEN DID YOU GET BACK, ANYWAY?

REALLY? WHAT?

12.

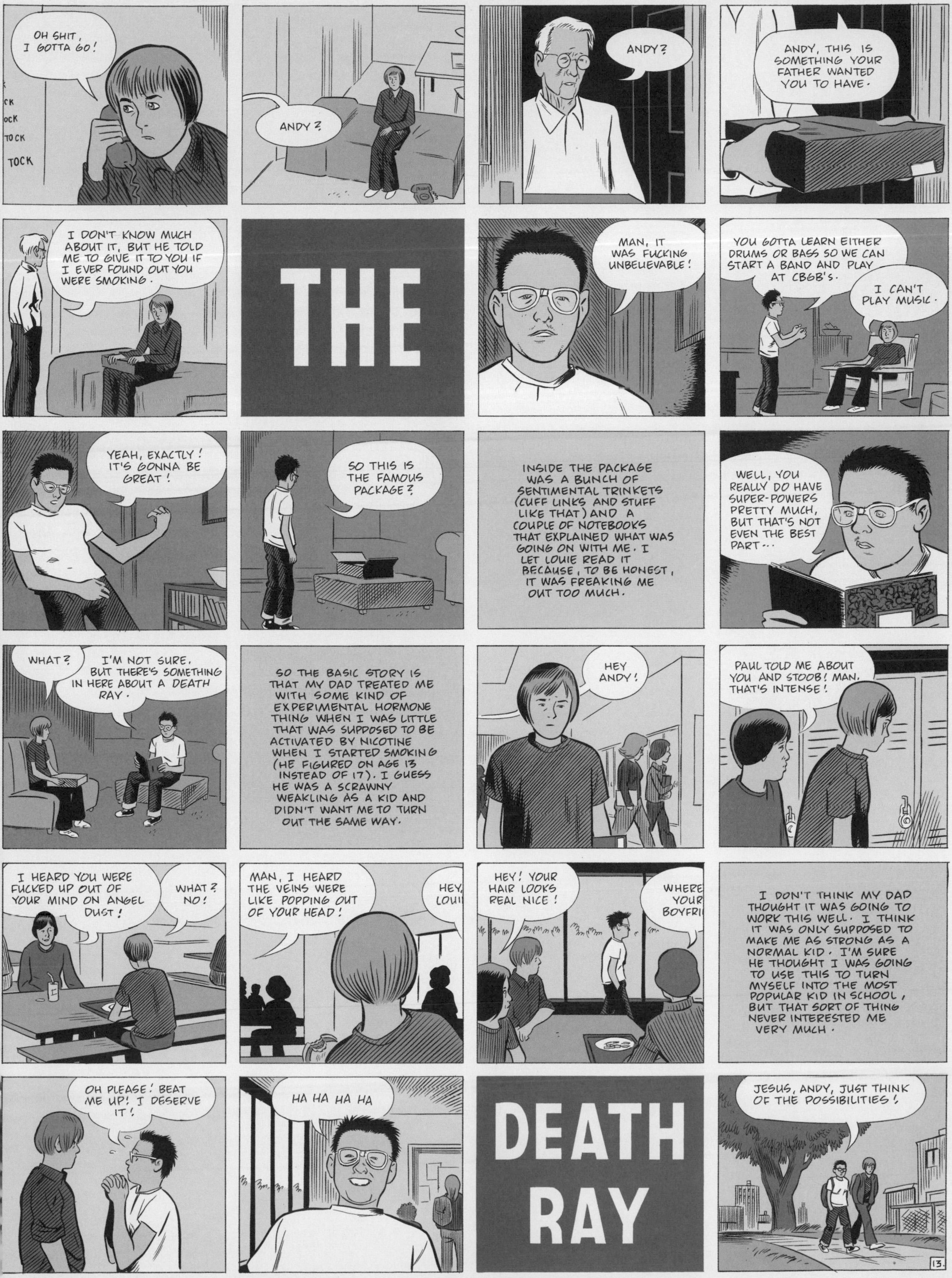
CK
OCK
TOCK
TOCK
OH SHIT, I GOTTA GO!
ANDY?
ANDY?
ANDY, THIS IS SOMETHING YOUR FATHER WANTED YOU TO HAVE.
I DON'T KNOW MUCH ABOUT IT, BUT HE TOLD ME TO GIVE IT TO YOU IF I EVER FOUND OUT YOU WERE SMOKING.
THE
MAN, IT WAS FUCKING UNBELIEVABLE!
YOU GOTTA LEARN EITHER DRUMS OR BASS SO WE CAN START A BAND AND PLAY AT CBGB'S.
I CAN'T PLAY MUSIC.
YEAH, EXACTLY! IT'S GONNA BE GREAT!
SO THIS IS THE FAMOUS PACKAGE?
INSIDE THE PACKAGE WAS A BUNCH OF SENTIMENTAL TRINKETS (CUFF LINKS AND STUFF LIKE THAT) AND A COUPLE OF NOTEBOOKS THAT EXPLAINED WHAT WAS GOING ON WITH ME. I LET LOUIE READ IT BECAUSE, TO BE HONEST, IT WAS FREAKING ME OUT TOO MUCH.
WELL, YOU REALLY DO HAVE SUPER-POWERS PRETTY MUCH, BUT THAT'S NOT EVEN THE BEST PART...
WHAT?
I'M NOT SURE. BUT THERE'S SOMETHING IN HERE ABOUT A DEATH RAY.
SO THE BASIC STORY IS THAT MY DAD TREATED ME WITH SOME KIND OF EXPERIMENTAL HORMONE THING WHEN I WAS LITTLE THAT WAS SUPPOSED TO BE ACTIVATED BY NICOTINE WHEN I STARTED SMOKING (HE FIGURED ON AGE 13 INSTEAD OF 17). I GUESS HE WAS A SCRAWNY WEAKLING AS A KID AND DIDN'T WANT ME TO TURN OUT THE SAME WAY.
HEY ANDY!
PAUL TOLD ME ABOUT YOU AND STOOB! MAN, THAT'S INTENSE!
I HEARD YOU WERE FUCKED UP OUT OF YOUR MIND ON ANGEL DUST!
WHAT? NO!
MAN, I HEARD THE VEINS WERE LIKE POPPING OUT OF YOUR HEAD!
HEY, LOUI
HEY! YOUR HAIR LOOKS REAL NICE!
WHERE YOUR BOYFRI
I DON'T THINK MY DAD THOUGHT IT WAS GOING TO WORK THIS WELL. I THINK IT WAS ONLY SUPPOSED TO MAKE ME AS STRONG AS A NORMAL KID. I'M SURE HE THOUGHT I WAS GOING TO USE THIS TO TURN MYSELF INTO THE MOST POPULAR KID IN SCHOOL, BUT THAT SORT OF THING NEVER INTERESTED ME VERY MUCH.
OH PLEASE! BEAT ME UP! I DESERVE IT!
HA HA HA HA
DEATH RAY
JESUS, ANDY, JUST THINK OF THE POSSIBILITIES!
13.

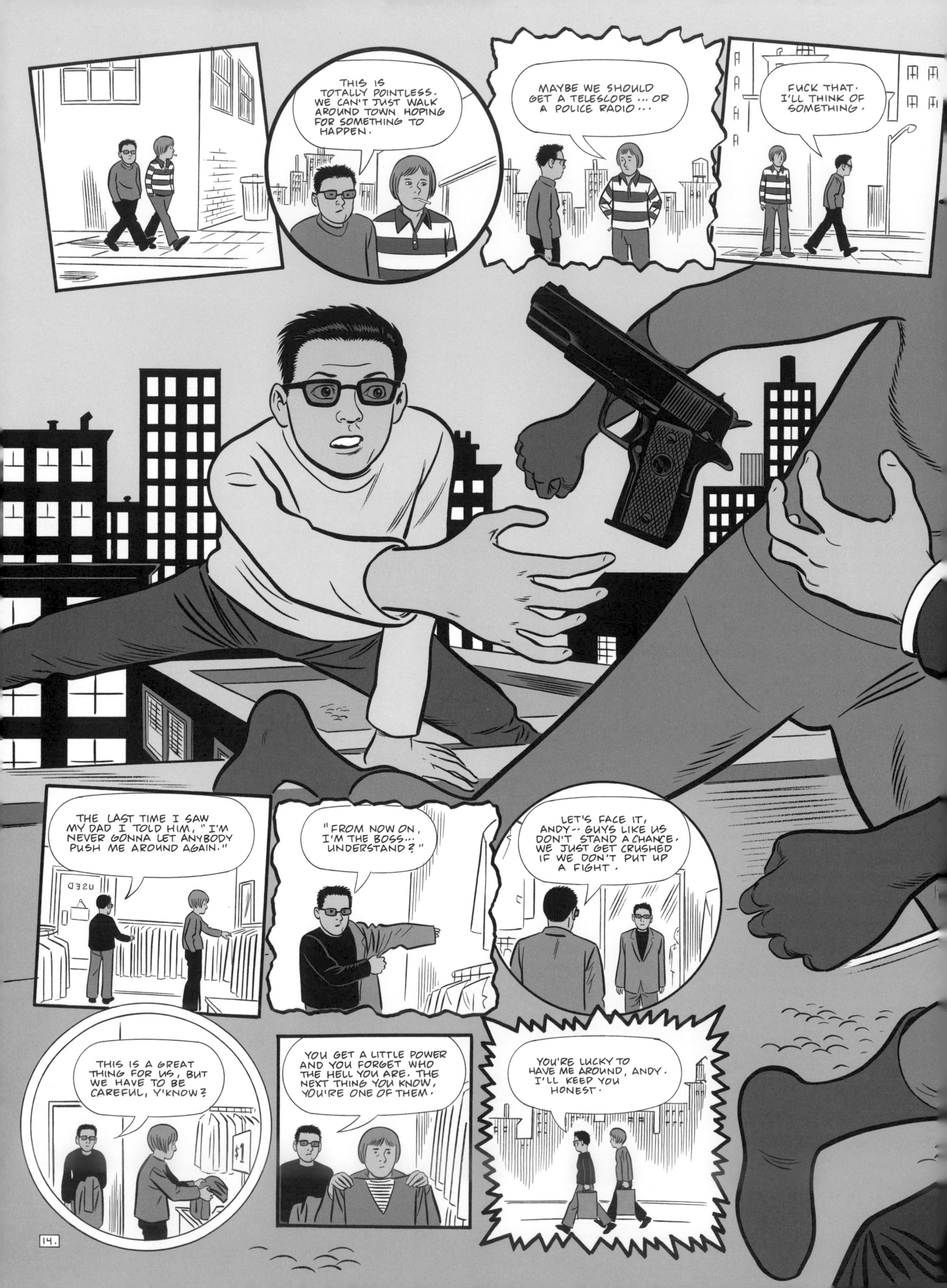

THIS IS TOTALLY POINTLESS. WE CAN'T JUST WALK AROUND TOWN HOPING FOR SOMETHING TO HAPPEN.
MAYBE WE SHOULD GET A TELESCOPE ... OR A POLICE RADIO ...
FUCK THAT. I'LL THINK OF SOMETHING.
THE LAST TIME I SAW MY DAD I TOLD HIM, "I'M NEVER GONNA LET ANYBODY PUSH ME AROUND AGAIN."
USED
"FROM NOW ON, I'M THE BOSS... UNDERSTAND?"
LET'S FACE IT, ANDY-- GUYS LIKE US DON'T STAND A CHANCE. WE JUST GET CRUSHED IF WE DON'T PUT UP A FIGHT.
THIS IS A GREAT THING FOR US, BUT WE HAVE TO BE CAREFUL, Y'KNOW?
$1
YOU GET A LITTLE POWER AND YOU FORGET WHO THE HELL YOU ARE. THE NEXT THING YOU KNOW, YOU'RE ONE OF THEM.
YOU'RE LUCKY TO HAVE ME AROUND, ANDY. I'LL KEEP YOU HONEST.

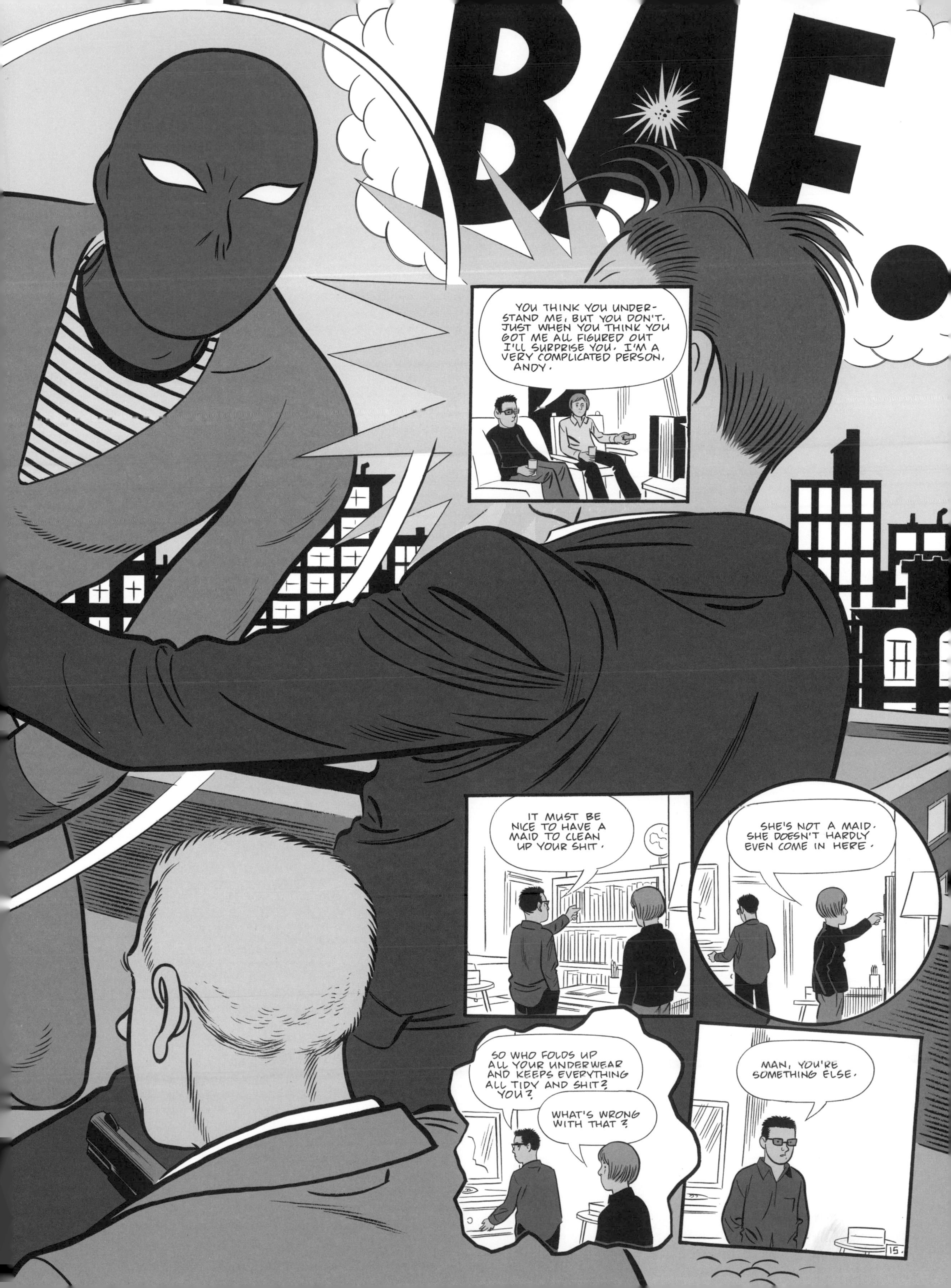
BAF.
YOU THINK YOU UNDERSTAND ME, BUT YOU DON'T. JUST WHEN YOU THINK YOU GOT ME ALL FIGURED OUT I'LL SURPRISE YOU. I'M A VERY COMPLICATED PERSON, ANDY.
IT MUST BE NICE TO HAVE A MAID TO CLEAN UP YOUR SHIT.
SHE'S NOT A MAID. SHE DOESN'T HARDLY EVEN COME IN HERE.
SO WHO FOLDS UP ALL YOUR UNDERWEAR AND KEEPS EVERYTHING ALL TIDY AND SHIT? YOU?
WHAT'S WRONG WITH THAT?
MAN, YOU'RE SOMETHING ELSE.
15.

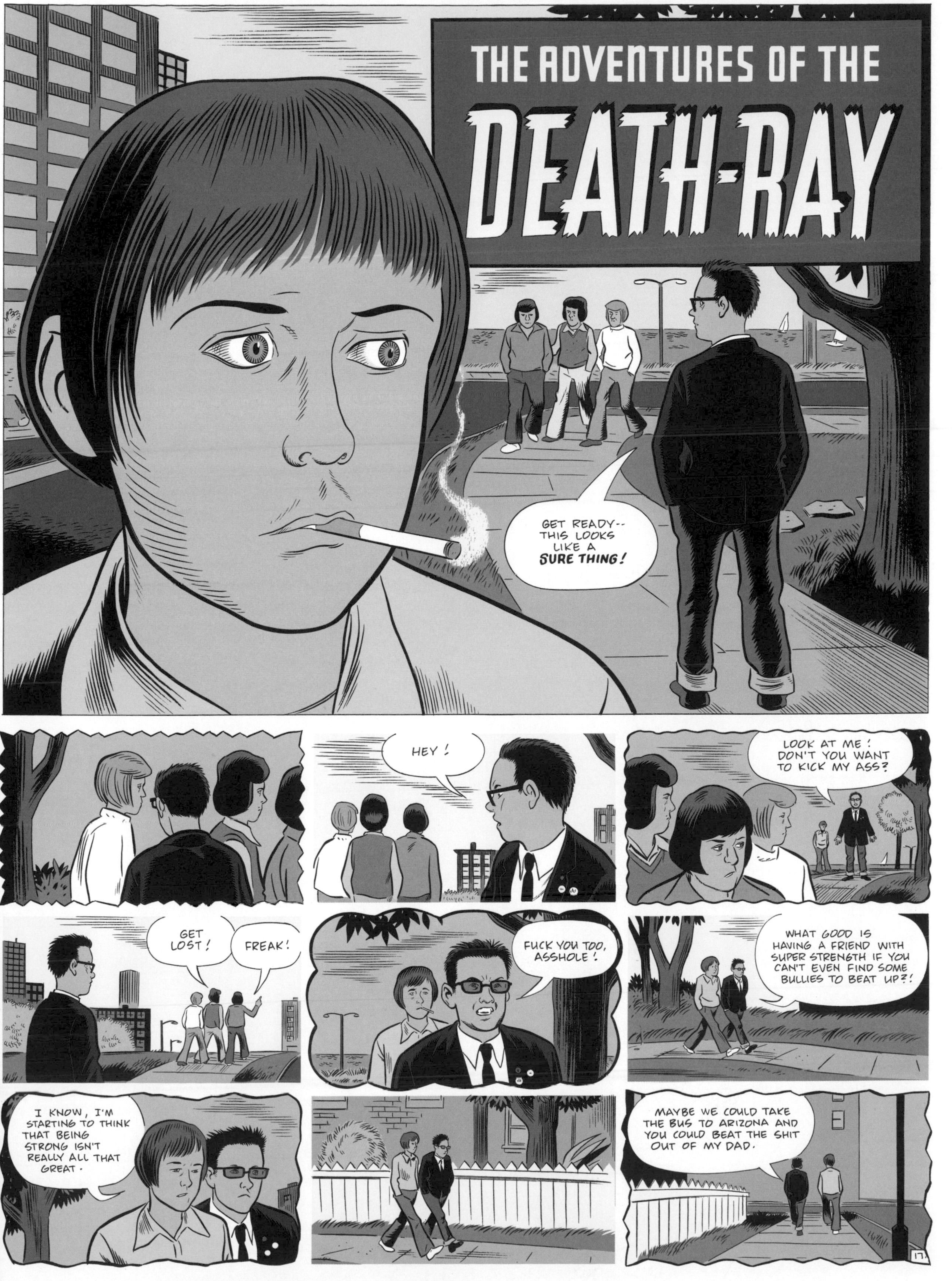
THE ADVENTURES OF THE
DEATH-RAY
GET READY-- THIS LOOKS LIKE A SURE THING!
HEY!
LOOK AT ME! DON'T YOU WANT TO KICK MY ASS?
GET LOST!
FREAK!
FUCK YOU TOO, ASSHOLE!
WHAT GOOD IS HAVING A FRIEND WITH SUPER STRENGTH IF YOU CAN'T EVEN FIND SOME BULLIES TO BEAT UP?!
I KNOW, I'M STARTING TO THINK THAT BEING STRONG ISN'T REALLY ALL THAT GREAT.
MAYBE WE COULD TAKE THE BUS TO ARIZONA AND YOU COULD BEAT THE SHIT OUT OF MY DAD.
17

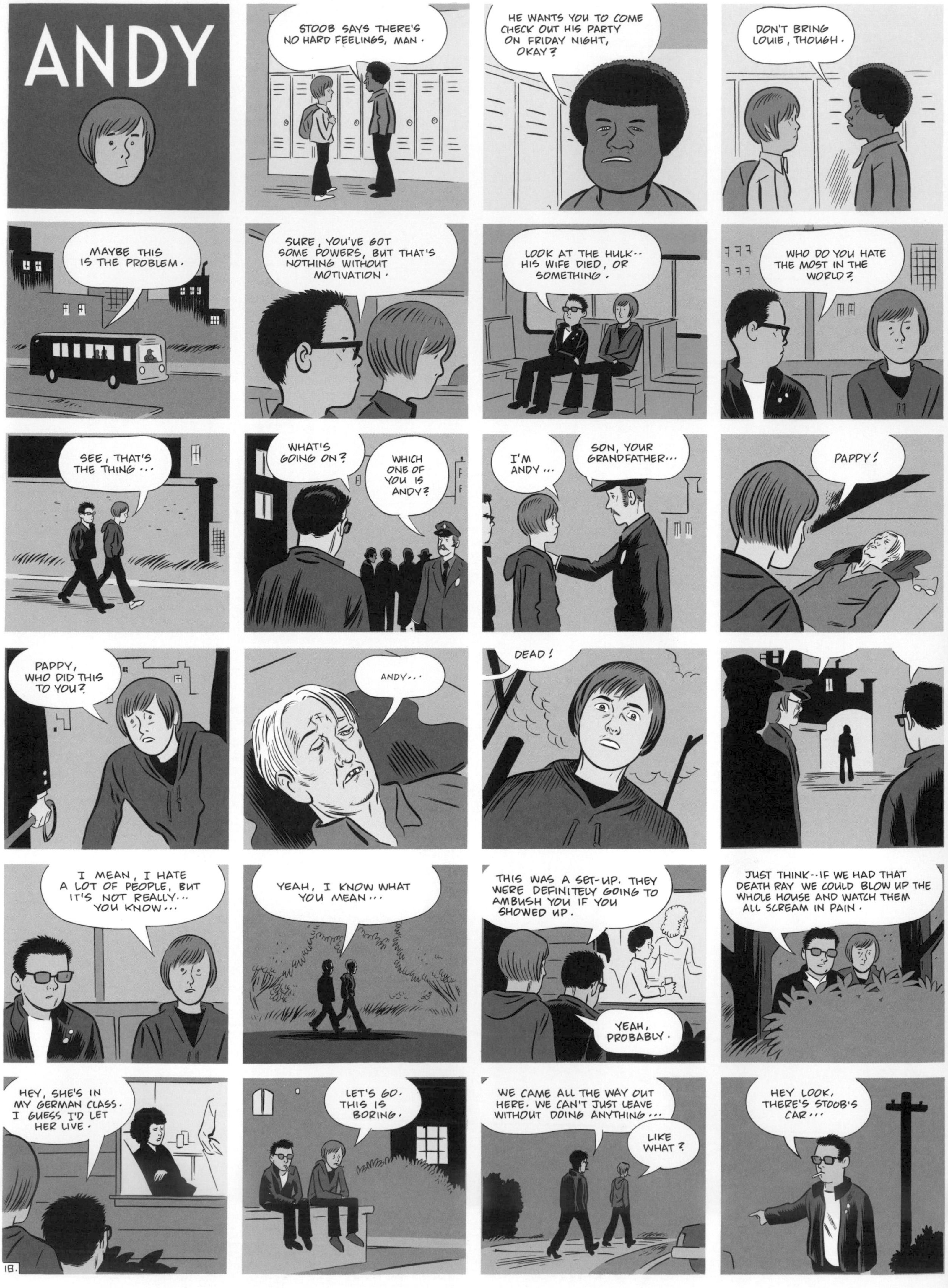
ANDY
STOOB SAYS THERE'S NO HARD FEELINGS, MAN.
HE WANTS YOU TO COME CHECK OUT HIS PARTY ON FRIDAY NIGHT, OKAY?
DON'T BRING LOUIE, THOUGH.
MAYBE THIS IS THE PROBLEM.
SURE, YOU'VE GOT SOME POWERS, BUT THAT'S NOTHING WITHOUT MOTIVATION.
LOOK AT THE HULK.. HIS WIFE DIED, OR SOMETHING.
WHO DO YOU HATE THE MOST IN THE WORLD?
SEE, THAT'S THE THING...
WHAT'S GOING ON?
WHICH ONE OF YOU IS ANDY?
I'M ANDY...
SON, YOUR GRANDFATHER...
PAPPY!
PAPPY, WHO DID THIS TO YOU?
ANDY...
DEAD!
I MEAN, I HATE A LOT OF PEOPLE, BUT IT'S NOT REALLY... YOU KNOW...
YEAH, I KNOW WHAT YOU MEAN...
THIS WAS A SET-UP. THEY WERE DEFINITELY GOING TO AMBUSH YOU IF YOU SHOWED UP.
YEAH, PROBABLY.
JUST THINK--IF WE HAD THAT DEATH RAY WE COULD BLOW UP THE WHOLE HOUSE AND WATCH THEM ALL SCREAM IN PAIN.
HEY, SHE'S IN MY GERMAN CLASS. I GUESS I'D LET HER LIVE.
LET'S GO. THIS IS BORING.
WE CAME ALL THE WAY OUT HERE. WE CAN'T JUST LEAVE WITHOUT DOING ANYTHING...
LIKE WHAT?
HEY LOOK, THERE'S STOOB'S CAR...

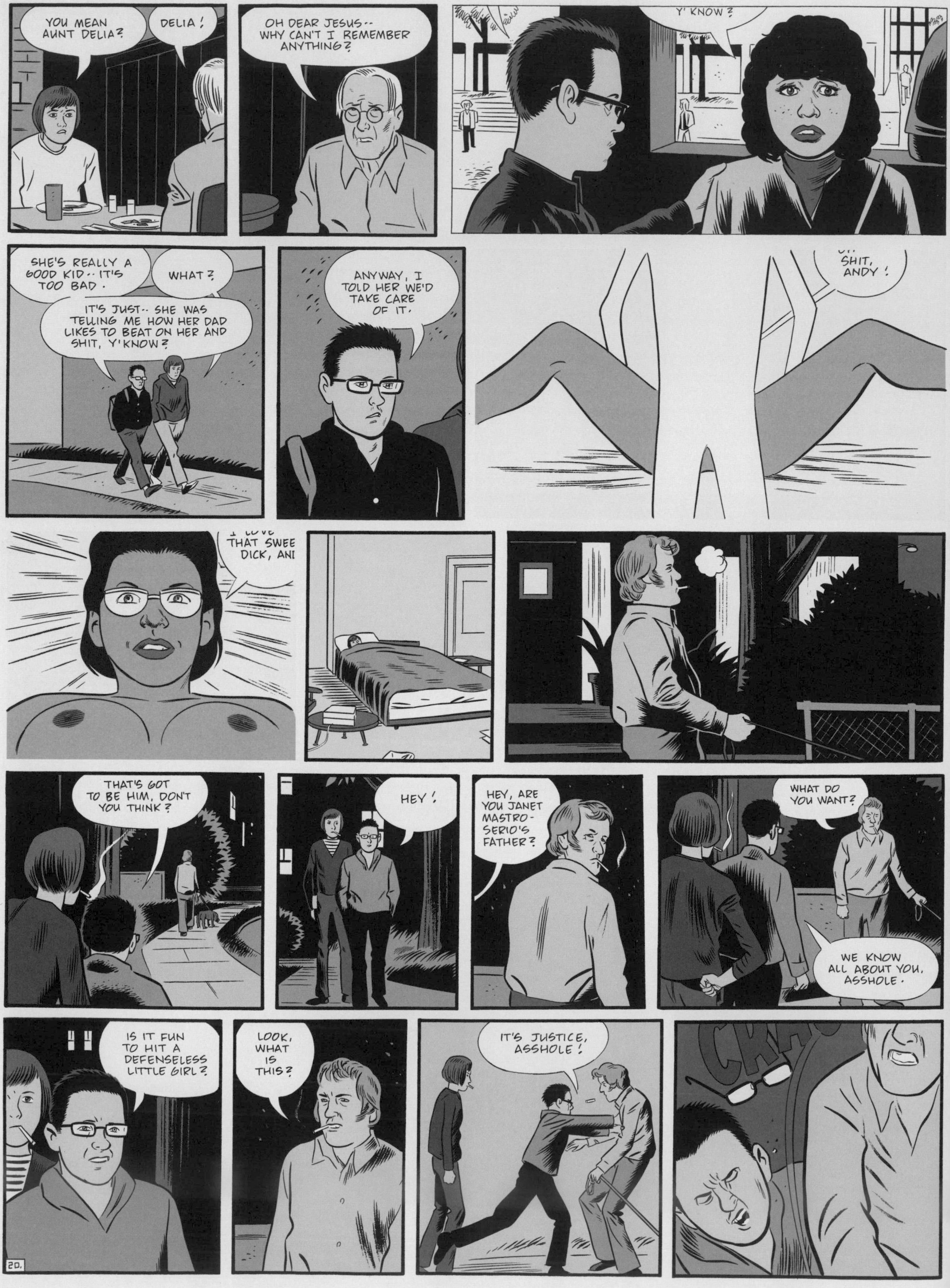

YOU MEAN AUNT DELIA?
DELIA!
OH DEAR JESUS -- WHY CAN'T I REMEMBER ANYTHING?
Y' KNOW?
SHE'S REALLY A GOOD KID -- IT'S TOO BAD.
WHAT?
IT'S JUST -- SHE WAS TELLING ME HOW HER DAD LIKES TO BEAT ON HER AND SHIT, Y'KNOW?
ANYWAY, I TOLD HER WE'D TAKE CARE OF IT.
SHIT, ANDY!
THAT SWEE
DICK, ANI
THAT'S GOT TO BE HIM, DON'T YOU THINK?
HEY!
HEY, ARE YOU JANET MASTRO-SERIO'S FATHER?
WHAT DO YOU WANT?
WE KNOW ALL ABOUT YOU, ASSHOLE.
IS IT FUN TO HIT A DEFENSELESS LITTLE GIRL?
LOOK, WHAT IS THIS?
IT'S JUSTICE, ASSHOLE!
20.

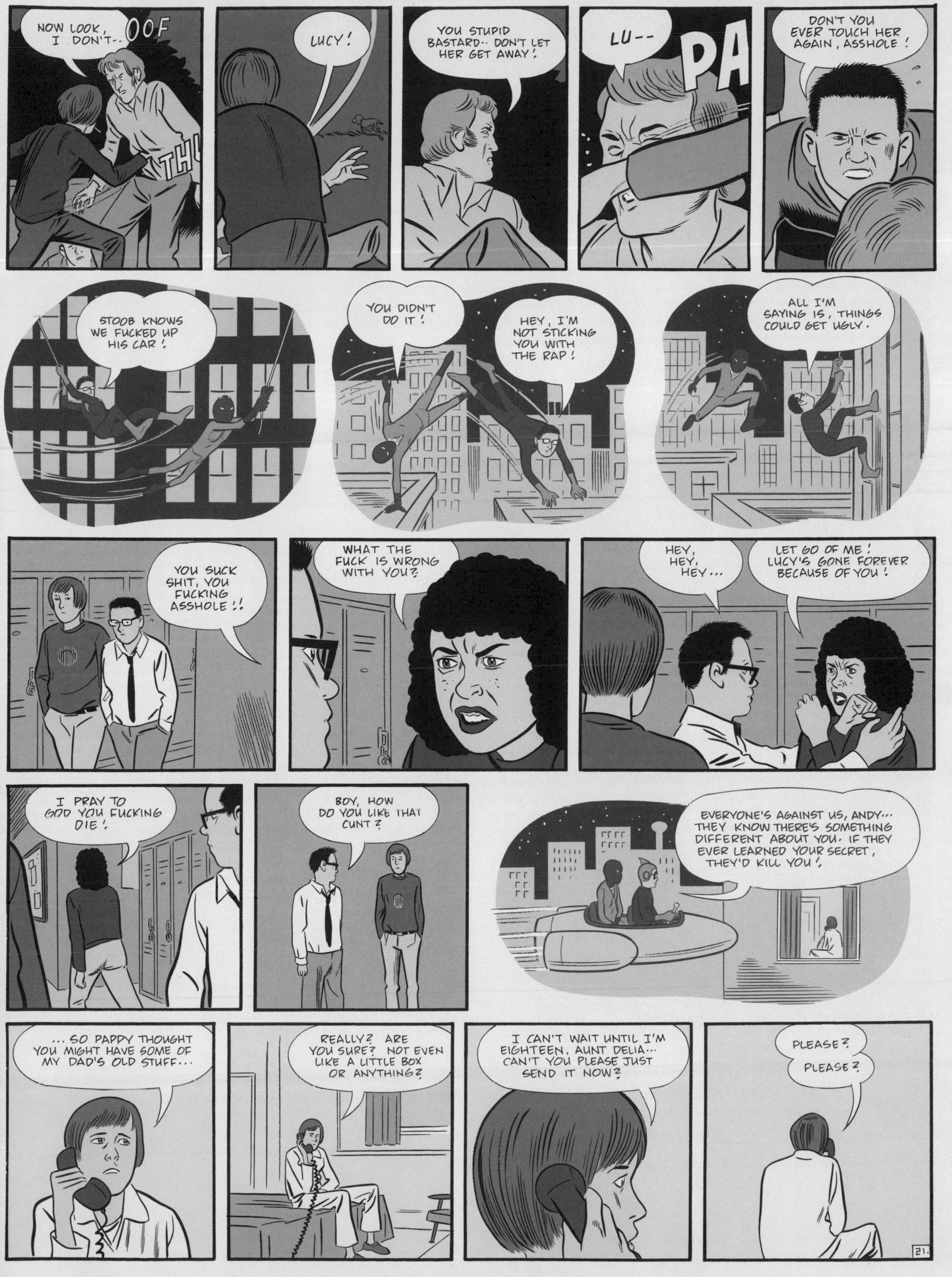
NOW LOOK, I DON'T--
OOF
THU
LUCY!
YOU STUPID BASTARD-- DON'T LET HER GET AWAY!
LU--
PA
DON'T YOU EVER TOUCH HER AGAIN, ASSHOLE!
STOOB KNOWS WE FUCKED UP HIS CAR!
YOU DIDN'T DO IT!
HEY, I'M NOT STICKING YOU WITH THE RAP!
ALL I'M SAYING IS, THINGS COULD GET UGLY.
YOU SUCK SHIT, YOU FUCKING ASSHOLE!!
WHAT THE FUCK IS WRONG WITH YOU?
HEY, HEY, HEY...
LET GO OF ME! LUCY'S GONE FOREVER BECAUSE OF YOU!
I PRAY TO GOD YOU FUCKING DIE!
BOY, HOW DO YOU LIKE THAT CUNT?
EVERYONE'S AGAINST US, ANDY... THEY KNOW THERE'S SOMETHING DIFFERENT ABOUT YOU. IF THEY EVER LEARNED YOUR SECRET, THEY'D KILL YOU!
... SO PAPPY THOUGHT YOU MIGHT HAVE SOME OF MY DAD'S OLD STUFF...
REALLY? ARE YOU SURE? NOT EVEN LIKE A LITTLE BOX OR ANYTHING?
I CAN'T WAIT UNTIL I'M EIGHTEEN, AUNT DELIA... CAN'T YOU PLEASE JUST SEND IT NOW?
PLEASE?
PLEASE?

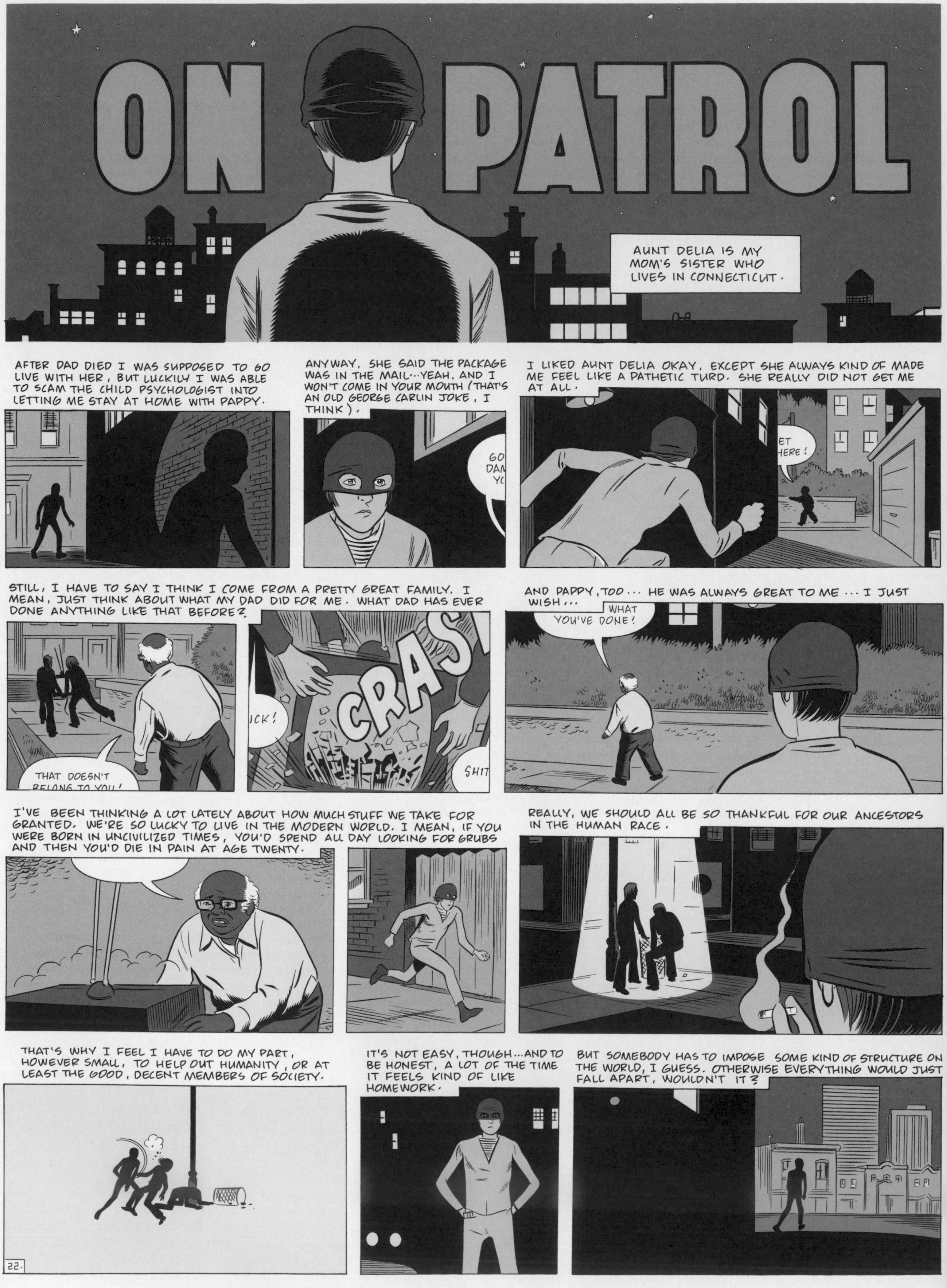
ON PATROL
AUNT DELIA IS MY MOM'S SISTER WHO LIVES IN CONNECTICUT.
AFTER DAD DIED I WAS SUPPOSED TO GO LIVE WITH HER, BUT LUCKILY I WAS ABLE TO SCAM THE CHILD PSYCHOLOGIST INTO LETTING ME STAY AT HOME WITH PAPPY.
ANYWAY, SHE SAID THE PACKAGE WAS IN THE MAIL... YEAH, AND I WON'T COME IN YOUR MOUTH (THAT'S AN OLD GEORGE CARLIN JOKE, I THINK).
I LIKED AUNT DELIA OKAY, EXCEPT SHE ALWAYS KIND OF MADE ME FEEL LIKE A PATHETIC TURD. SHE REALLY DID NOT GET ME AT ALL.
STILL, I HAVE TO SAY I THINK I COME FROM A PRETTY GREAT FAMILY. I MEAN, JUST THINK ABOUT WHAT MY DAD DID FOR ME. WHAT DAD HAS EVER DONE ANYTHING LIKE THAT BEFORE?
THAT DOESN'T BELONG TO YOU!
CRASH
SHIT
AND PAPPY, TOO... HE WAS ALWAYS GREAT TO ME... I JUST WISH...
WHAT YOU'VE DONE!
I'VE BEEN THINKING A LOT LATELY ABOUT HOW MUCH STUFF WE TAKE FOR GRANTED. WE'RE SO LUCKY TO LIVE IN THE MODERN WORLD. I MEAN, IF YOU WERE BORN IN UNCIVILIZED TIMES, YOU'D SPEND ALL DAY LOOKING FOR GRUBS AND THEN YOU'D DIE IN PAIN AT AGE TWENTY.
REALLY, WE SHOULD ALL BE SO THANKFUL FOR OUR ANCESTORS IN THE HUMAN RACE.
THAT'S WHY I FEEL I HAVE TO DO MY PART, HOWEVER SMALL, TO HELP OUT HUMANITY, OR AT LEAST THE GOOD, DECENT MEMBERS OF SOCIETY.
22.
IT'S NOT EASY, THOUGH... AND TO BE HONEST, A LOT OF THE TIME IT FEELS KIND OF LIKE HOMEWORK.
BUT SOMEBODY HAS TO IMPOSE SOME KIND OF STRUCTURE ON THE WORLD, I GUESS. OTHERWISE EVERYTHING WOULD JUST FALL APART, WOULDN'T IT?

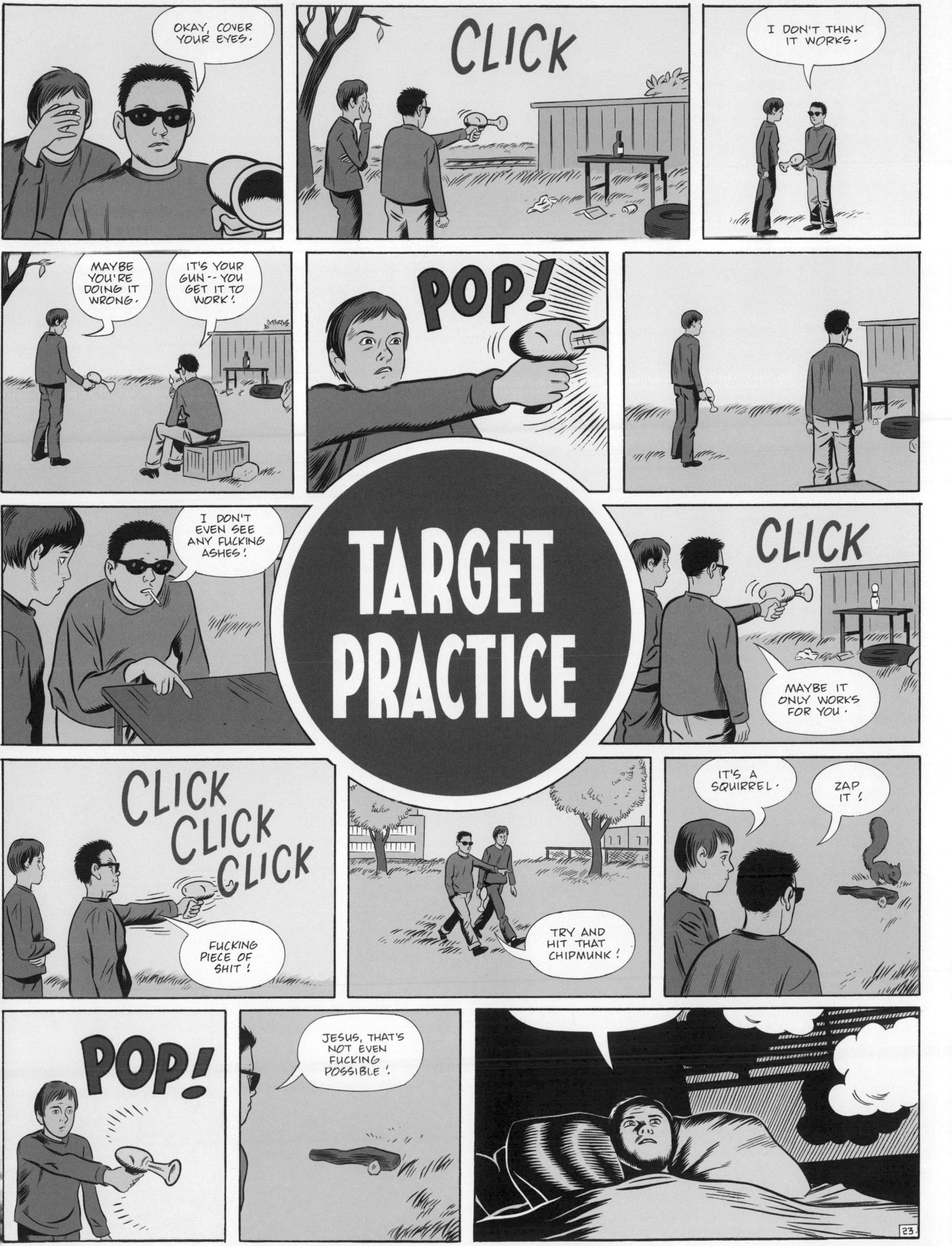

OKAY, COVER YOUR EYES.
CLICK
I DON'T THINK IT WORKS.
MAYBE YOU'RE DOING IT WRONG.
IT'S YOUR GUN -- YOU GET IT TO WORK!
POP!
TARGET PRACTICE
I DON'T EVEN SEE ANY FUCKING ASHES!
CLICK
MAYBE IT ONLY WORKS FOR YOU.
CLICK CLICK CLICK
FUCKING PIECE OF SHIT!
TRY AND HIT THAT CHIPMUNK!
IT'S A SQUIRREL.
ZAP IT!
POP!
JESUS, THAT'S NOT EVEN FUCKING POSSIBLE!
23.

SONNY

I can feel myself changing -- or maybe not changing, exactly, but coming to realize who I am as a person.

Really I'm kind of an All-American type.. A modest guy with common sense who knows the difference between right and wrong.

I'm a straight-shooter and a stand-up guy. I value honesty, integrity, and above all else, loyalty.

SO OBVIOUSLY YOU SHOULDN'T TELL ANYONE ABOUT THE GUN, OKAY?

HOLY SHIT-- CHECK IT OUT!

YEAH, SO WHEN I WAS IN NEW YORK I MET THESE GUYS AT MAX'S ···YEAH, JOHNNY WAS A REAL COOL GUY, Y'KNOW?

HE'S NOT JUST SOME ASSHOLE ROCK STAR, HE'S LIKE A TOTALLY REGULAR GUY.

PATRIOTIC MARCHES
THE MUSICAL LEGACY
MILITARY AMERICA

YEAH, HE TOLD ME I COULD COME BACKSTAGE ANY TIME THEY'RE IN TOWN, AND WHEN I GET MY BAND TOGETHER

OF COURSE I WON'T TELL ANYBODY ABOUT THE GUN.

LOOK, THERE'S ANOTHER SQUIRREL FOR YOU TO INCINERATE.

DON'T YOU EVER SAY ANYTHING LIKE THAT AGAIN - YOU HEAR ME? IT'S NOT A JOKE.

HERE BOY···
C'MERE!

C'MERE, I'VE GOT SOMETHING FOR YOU···

OR WHAT?

OR WHAT WHAT?
DON'T EVER SAY ANYTHING LIKE THAT AGAIN OR I'LL WHAT?

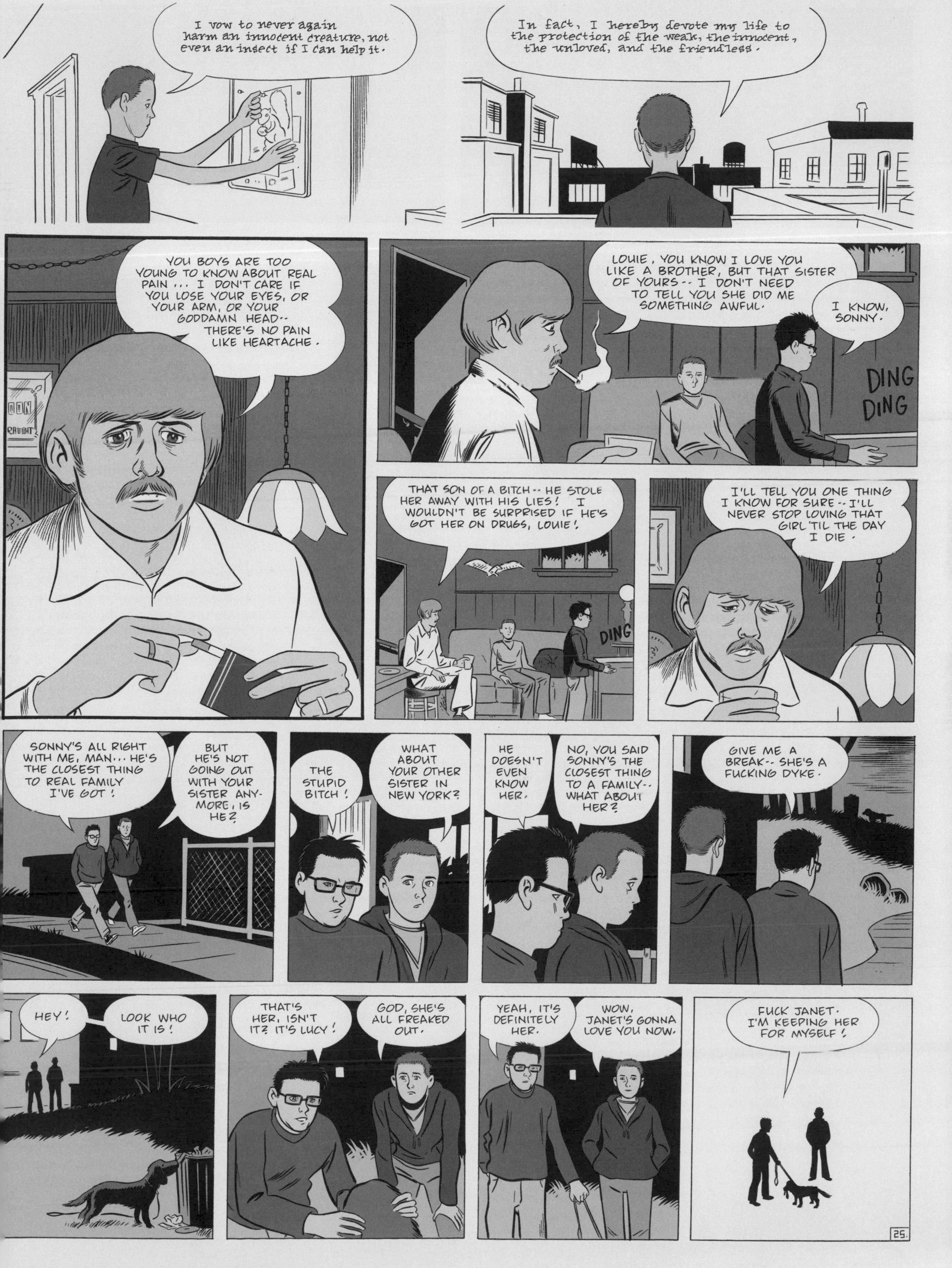

I vow to never again harm an innocent creature, not even an insect if I can help it.
In fact, I hereby devote my life to the protection of the weak, the innocent, the unloved, and the friendless.
YOU BOYS ARE TOO YOUNG TO KNOW ABOUT REAL PAIN... I DON'T CARE IF YOU LOSE YOUR EYES, OR YOUR ARM, OR YOUR GODDAMN HEAD-- THERE'S NO PAIN LIKE HEARTACHE.
LOUIE, YOU KNOW I LOVE YOU LIKE A BROTHER, BUT THAT SISTER OF YOURS-- I DON'T NEED TO TELL YOU SHE DID ME SOMETHING AWFUL.
I KNOW, SONNY.
DING DING
THAT SON OF A BITCH-- HE STOLE HER AWAY WITH HIS LIES! I WOULDN'T BE SURPRISED IF HE'S GOT HER ON DRUGS, LOUIE!
DING
I'LL TELL YOU ONE THING I KNOW FOR SURE-- I'LL NEVER STOP LOVING THAT GIRL 'TIL THE DAY I DIE.
SONNY'S ALL RIGHT WITH ME, MAN... HE'S THE CLOSEST THING TO REAL FAMILY I'VE GOT!
BUT HE'S NOT GOING OUT WITH YOUR SISTER ANY-MORE, IS HE?
THE STUPID BITCH!
WHAT ABOUT YOUR OTHER SISTER IN NEW YORK?
HE DOESN'T EVEN KNOW HER.
NO, YOU SAID SONNY'S THE CLOSEST THING TO A FAMILY-- WHAT ABOUT HER?
GIVE ME A BREAK-- SHE'S A FUCKING DYKE.
HEY!
LOOK WHO IT IS!
THAT'S HER, ISN'T IT? IT'S LUCY!
GOD, SHE'S ALL FREAKED OUT.
YEAH, IT'S DEFINITELY HER.
WOW, JANET'S GONNA LOVE YOU NOW.
FUCK JANET. I'M KEEPING HER FOR MYSELF!

There was this tree with these big white berries growing on it, and as soon as a person ate one they would start to disappear.

This process seemed to be both physically painful and super-terrifying.

I was so scared of the tree, which I guess was supposed to be in my back yard, that I didn't even want to go outside.

I stayed in my room for a long time and it seemed pretty safe until I started to notice these weird little clouds floating up around the ceiling. I was able to get rid of them by waving a broom around, but after a few hours they came back even stronger.

I went to make a break for it, but outside the door was pure whiteness. It filled up the room and blanked it out. I've never been so scared.

I woke up totally drenched. No matter what I did, I couldn't get away from the nothingness.

Later that night I had another dream. In this one I was having sex with my housekeeper.

It's funny, but I never even see you naked in my dreams.

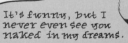

I guess my brain has too much respect for you.

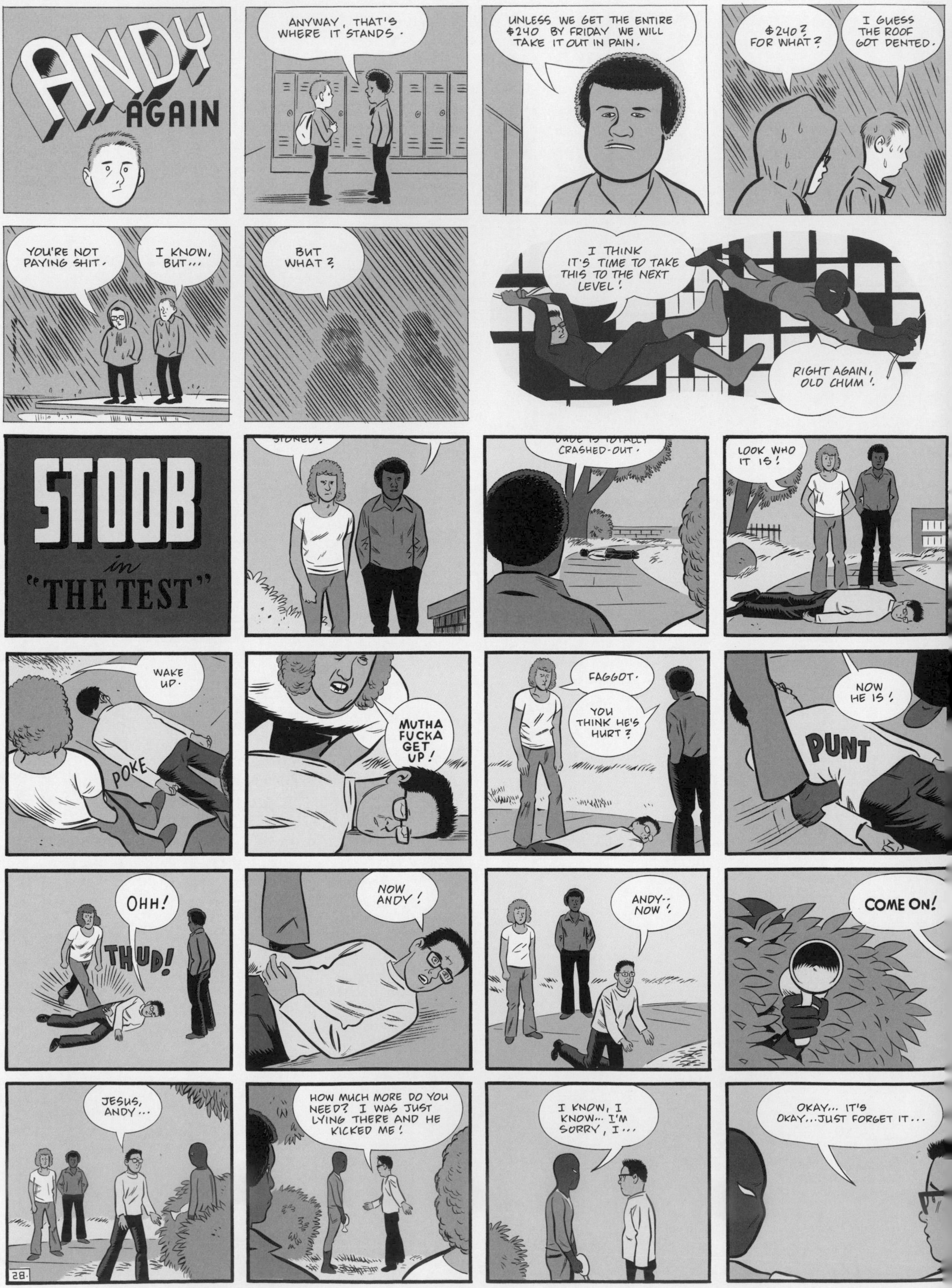
ANDY AGAIN
ANYWAY, THAT'S WHERE IT STANDS.
UNLESS WE GET THE ENTIRE $240 BY FRIDAY WE WILL TAKE IT OUT IN PAIN.
$240? FOR WHAT?
I GUESS THE ROOF GOT DENTED.
YOU'RE NOT PAYING SHIT.
I KNOW, BUT...
BUT WHAT?
I THINK IT'S TIME TO TAKE THIS TO THE NEXT LEVEL!
RIGHT AGAIN, OLD CHUM!
STOOB in "THE TEST"
CRASHED-OUT.
LOOK WHO IT IS!
WAKE UP.
POKE
MUTHA FUCKA GET UP!
FAGGOT.
YOU THINK HE'S HURT?
NOW HE IS!
PUNT
OHH!
THUD!
NOW ANDY!
ANDY-- NOW!
COME ON!
JESUS, ANDY...
HOW MUCH MORE DO YOU NEED? I WAS JUST LYING THERE AND HE KICKED ME!
I KNOW, I KNOW... I'M SORRY, I...
OKAY... IT'S OKAY... JUST FORGET IT...

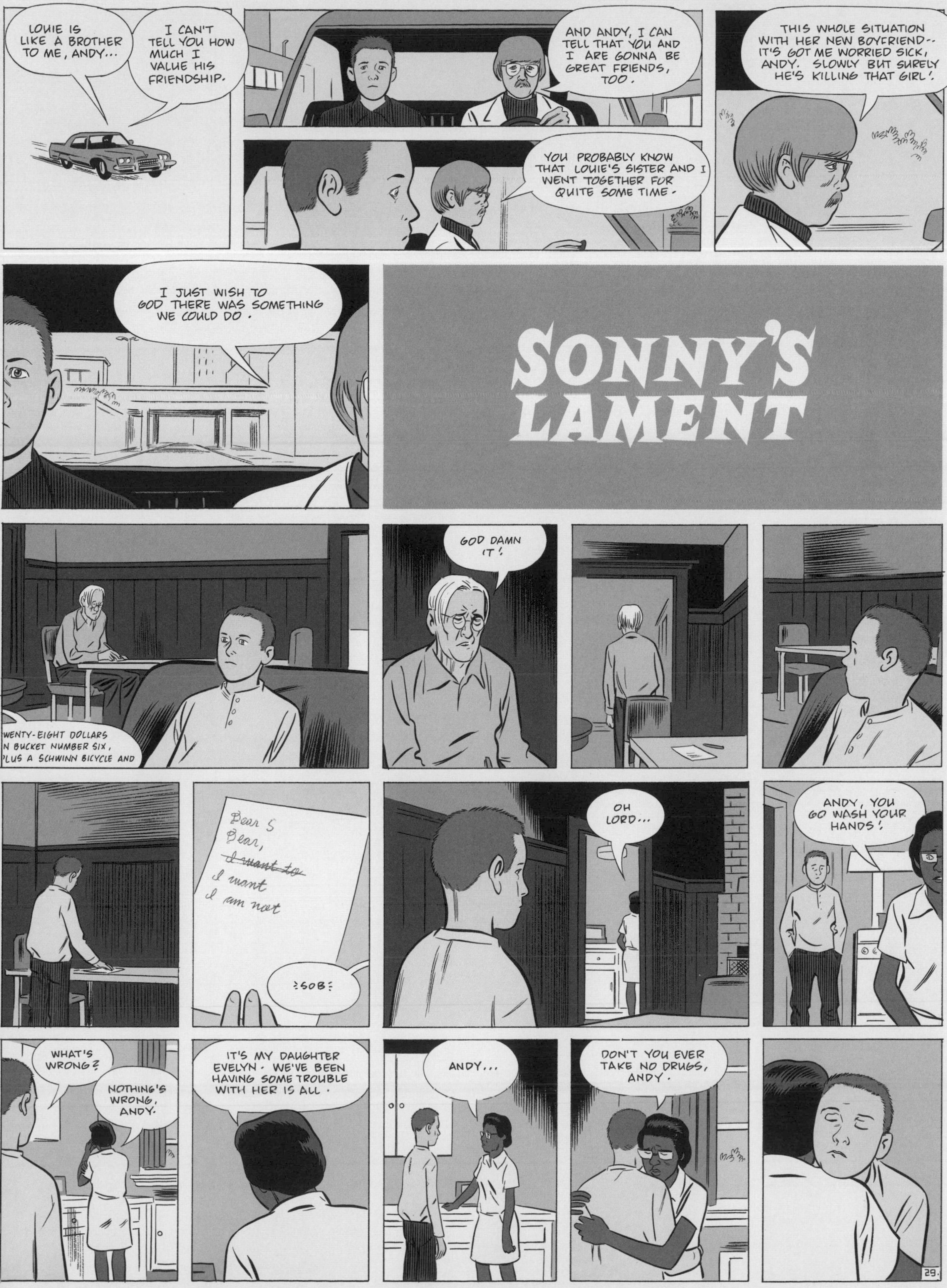

LOUIE IS LIKE A BROTHER TO ME, ANDY...
I CAN'T TELL YOU HOW MUCH I VALUE HIS FRIENDSHIP.
AND ANDY, I CAN TELL THAT YOU AND I ARE GONNA BE GREAT FRIENDS, TOO.
YOU PROBABLY KNOW THAT LOUIE'S SISTER AND I WENT TOGETHER FOR QUITE SOME TIME.
THIS WHOLE SITUATION WITH HER NEW BOYFRIEND-- IT'S GOT ME WORRIED SICK, ANDY. SLOWLY BUT SURELY HE'S KILLING THAT GIRL!
I JUST WISH TO GOD THERE WAS SOMETHING WE COULD DO.
SONNY'S LAMENT
WENTY-EIGHT DOLLARS
N BUCKET NUMBER SIX,
PLUS A SCHWINN BICYCLE AND
GOD DAMN IT!
Dear S
Dear,
I want to
I want
I am not
SOB
OH LORD...
ANDY, YOU GO WASH YOUR HANDS!
WHAT'S WRONG?
NOTHING'S WRONG, ANDY.
IT'S MY DAUGHTER EVELYN. WE'VE BEEN HAVING SOME TROUBLE WITH HER IS ALL.
ANDY...
DON'T YOU EVER TAKE NO DRUGS, ANDY.

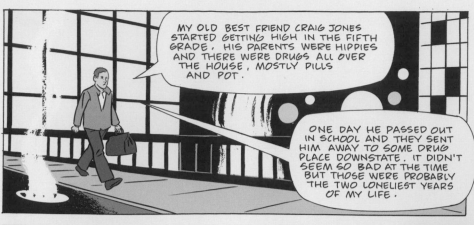

MY OLD BEST FRIEND CRAIG JONES STARTED GETTING HIGH IN THE FIFTH GRADE. HIS PARENTS WERE HIPPIES AND THERE WERE DRUGS ALL OVER THE HOUSE, MOSTLY PILLS AND POT.

ONE DAY HE PASSED OUT IN SCHOOL AND THEY SENT HIM AWAY TO SOME DRUG PLACE DOWNSTATE. IT DIDN'T SEEM SO BAD AT THE TIME BUT THOSE WERE PROBABLY THE TWO LONELIEST YEARS OF MY LIFE.

WHEN HE CAME BACK HE WAS ALL OF A SUDDEN REALLY POPULAR, BUT HE STILL USED TO COME OVER AND HANG OUT WITH ME. WE WOULD JUST WATCH TV OR PLAY NERF BASKETBALL AND IT WAS PRETTY MUCH LIKE OLD TIMES.

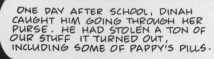

ONE DAY AFTER SCHOOL, DINAH CAUGHT HIM GOING THROUGH HER PURSE. HE HAD STOLEN A TON OF OUR STUFF IT TURNED OUT, INCLUDING SOME OF PAPPY'S PILLS.

I WOULD STILL SEE HIM AROUND SCHOOL AFTER THAT, BUT HE WAS PART OF A WHOLE DIFFERENT CROWD. A FEW YEARS LATER HE DROPPED OUT AND I NEVER SAW HIM AGAIN.

WE'RE THE COOLEST GUYS IN THE WORLD.

MAYBE SO.

IT'S NOT AN OPINION, IT'S A FACT.

DID YOU TELL SONNY ABOUT THE GUN?

NO WAY. I'M TOTALLY LOYAL TO YOU, ANDY.

NO WAY IN HELL.

AND ANYWAY, WE'RE NOT DOING IT FOR SONNY, WE'RE DOING IT FOR AMERICA!

Y'KNOW?

NOBODY WILL EVER KNOW A THING, ANDY.

FOR ALL THEY KNOW, HE JUST MOVED AWAY.

FOR ALL THEY KNOW, HE JUST WENT ON VACATION. THEY'LL NEVER--

POP

FEETS DON'T FAIL ME NOW!

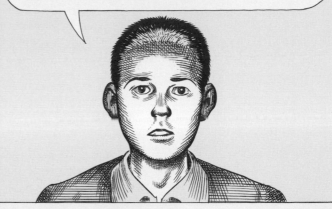

YOU'D THINK SOMETHING LIKE THAT WOULD FREAK ME OUT, BUT I HARDLY GAVE IT ANOTHER THOUGHT. I GUESS I'M GROWING UP. I MEAN, ADULTS HAVE TO DEAL WITH TOUGH DECISIONS EVERY DAY. NOT THAT IT'S SOMETHING I TAKE LIGHTLY, AND I HOPE TO GOD I NEVER HAVE TO DO IT AGAIN EVER, BUT...

I DIDN'T THINK HE HAD IT IN HIM. I WAS JUST-- I DON'T KNOW, I JUST DIDN'T EXPECT IT. I MEAN, HE WAS MORE UPSET ABOUT THE CHIPMUNK! I GUESS I SHOULD BE GLAD HE'S MY FRIEND, BUT JESUS CHRIST, ANDY!

THANKS, DUDE.

SO I'VE BEEN DOING SOME THINKING, ANDY...

'SCUSE ME, BOYS...

ANDY, BUDDY-- CAN I BORROW YOU FOR A SEC?

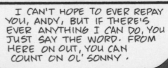

ANDY, I DON'T KNOW THE WHOLE STORY -- I'M PRETTY SURE I DON'T WANT TO KNOW...

I CAN'T HOPE TO EVER REPAY YOU, ANDY, BUT IF THERE'S EVER ANYTHING I CAN DO, YOU JUST SAY THE WORD. FROM HERE ON OUT, YOU CAN COUNT ON OL' SONNY.

I MEAN IT, BUDDY.

SO I THINK WE SHOULD STASH THE GUN SOMEWHERE... Y'KNOW, JUST FOR A WHILE UNTIL WE FIGURE OUT WHAT WE'RE DOING.

LOOK, LOUIE... I'M THE BOSS NOW.

OH, OKAY ANDY. WHAT EVER YOU SAY.

SO WHO ARE YOU GONNA KILL NEXT?

WHAT'S THAT SUPPOSED TO MEAN?

NOTHING... I JUST THOUGHT...

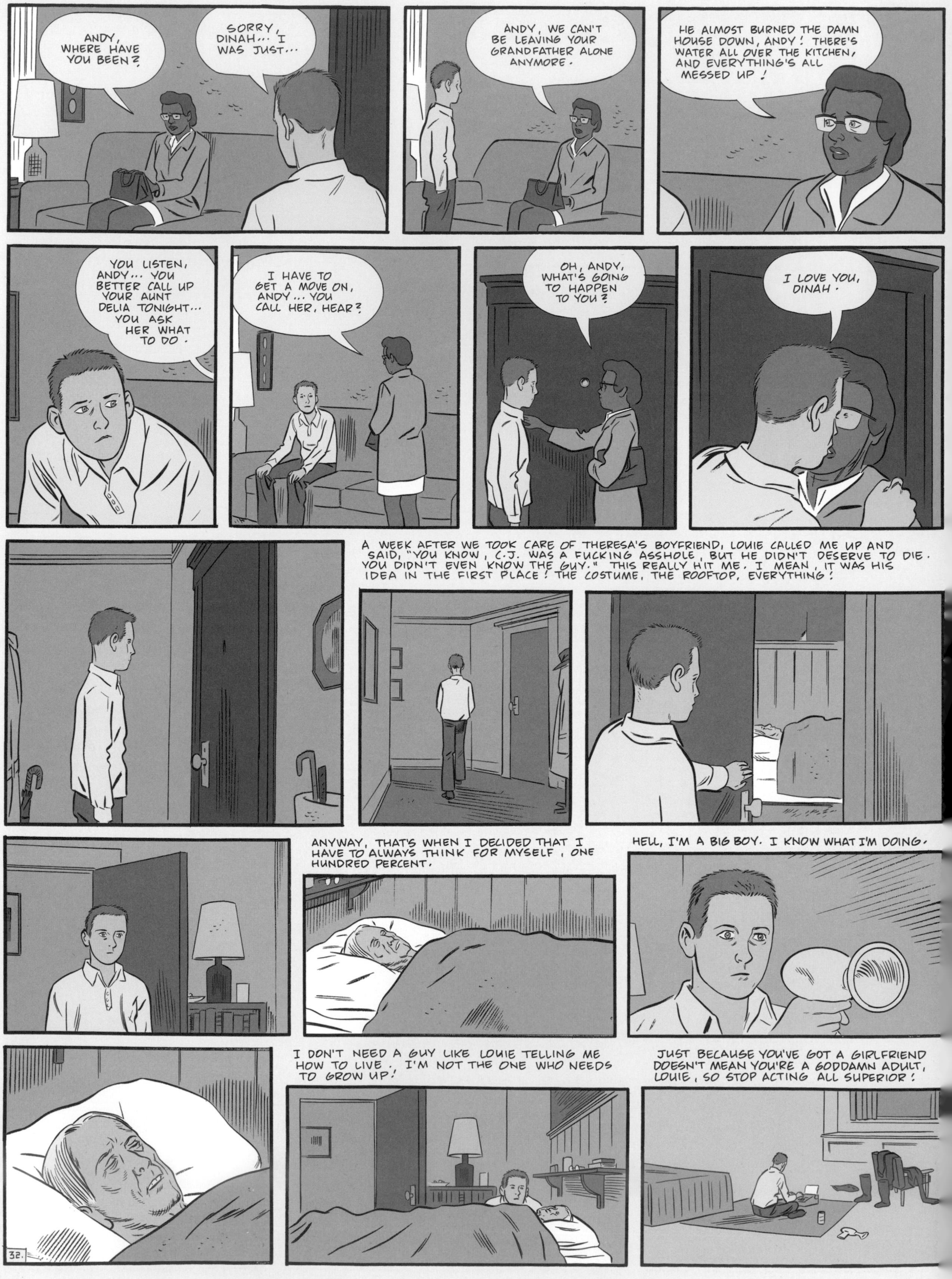
ANDY, WHERE HAVE YOU BEEN?
SORRY, DINAH... I WAS JUST...
ANDY, WE CAN'T BE LEAVING YOUR GRANDFATHER ALONE ANYMORE.
HE ALMOST BURNED THE DAMN HOUSE DOWN, ANDY! THERE'S WATER ALL OVER THE KITCHEN, AND EVERYTHING'S ALL MESSED UP!
YOU LISTEN, ANDY... YOU BETTER CALL UP YOUR AUNT DELIA TONIGHT... YOU ASK HER WHAT TO DO.
I HAVE TO GET A MOVE ON, ANDY... YOU CALL HER, HEAR?
OH, ANDY, WHAT'S GOING TO HAPPEN TO YOU?
I LOVE YOU, DINAH.
A WEEK AFTER WE TOOK CARE OF THERESA'S BOYFRIEND, LOUIE CALLED ME UP AND SAID, "YOU KNOW, C.J. WAS A FUCKING ASSHOLE, BUT HE DIDN'T DESERVE TO DIE. YOU DIDN'T EVEN KNOW THE GUY." THIS REALLY HIT ME. I MEAN, IT WAS HIS IDEA IN THE FIRST PLACE! THE COSTUME, THE ROOFTOP, EVERYTHING!
ANYWAY, THAT'S WHEN I DECIDED THAT I HAVE TO ALWAYS THINK FOR MYSELF, ONE HUNDRED PERCENT.
HELL, I'M A BIG BOY. I KNOW WHAT I'M DOING.
I DON'T NEED A GUY LIKE LOUIE TELLING ME HOW TO LIVE. I'M NOT THE ONE WHO NEEDS TO GROW UP!
JUST BECAUSE YOU'VE GOT A GIRLFRIEND DOESN'T MEAN YOU'RE A GODDAMN ADULT, LOUIE, SO STOP ACTING ALL SUPERIOR!

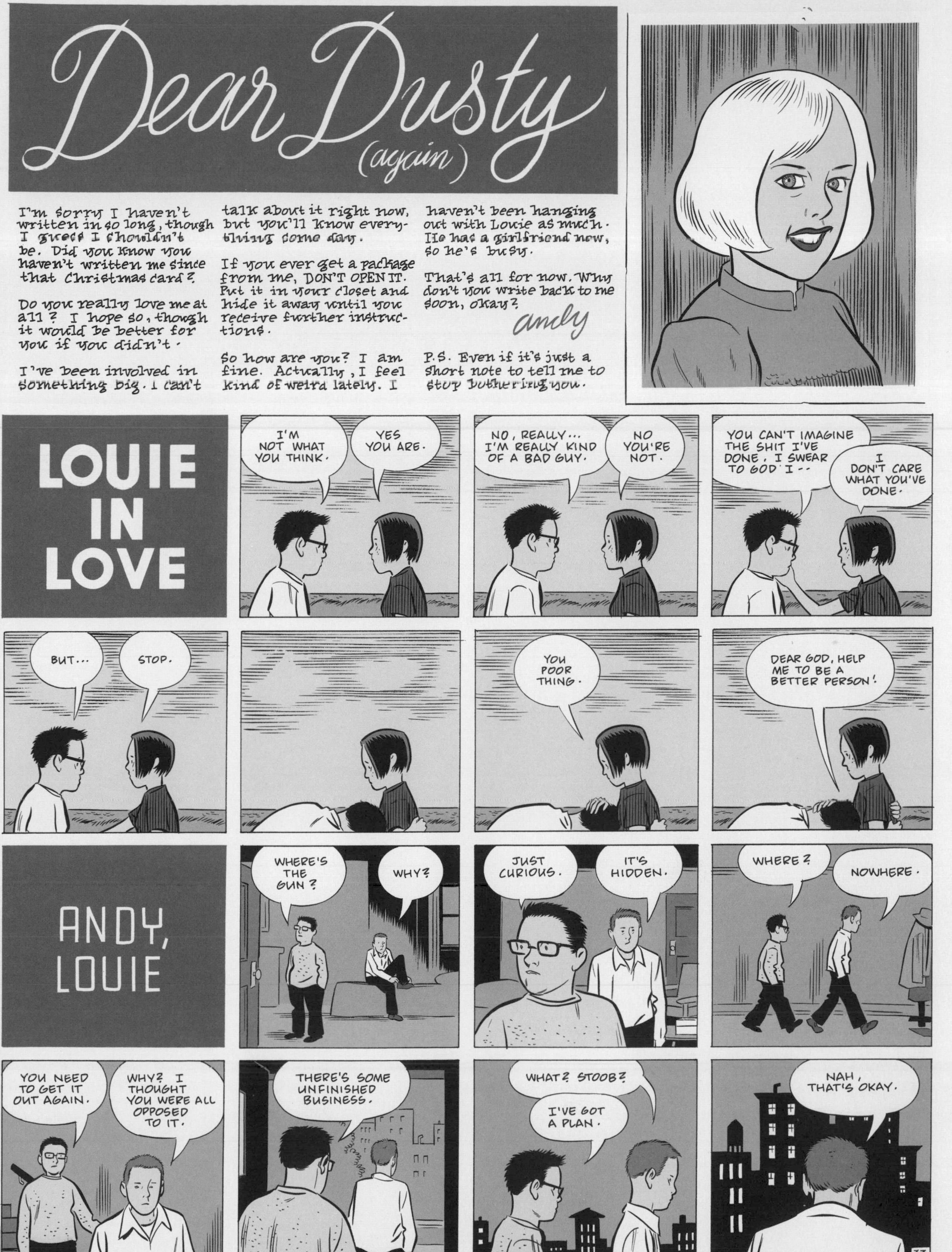
Dear Dusty
(again)
I'm sorry I haven't written in so long, though I guess I shouldn't be. Did you know you haven't written me since that Christmas card?
Do you really love me at all? I hope so, though it would be better for you if you didn't.
I've been involved in something big. I can't talk about it right now, but you'll know everything some day.
If you ever get a package from me, DON'T OPEN IT. Put it in your closet and hide it away until you receive further instructions.
So how are you? I am fine. Actually, I feel kind of weird lately. I haven't been hanging out with Louie as much. He has a girlfriend now, so he's busy.
That's all for now. Why don't you write back to me soon, okay?
andy
P.S. Even if it's just a short note to tell me to stop bothering you.
LOUIE IN LOVE
I'M NOT WHAT YOU THINK.
YES YOU ARE.
NO, REALLY... I'M REALLY KIND OF A BAD GUY.
NO YOU'RE NOT.
YOU CAN'T IMAGINE THE SHIT I'VE DONE. I SWEAR TO GOD I--
I DON'T CARE WHAT YOU'VE DONE.
BUT...
STOP.
YOU POOR THING.
DEAR GOD, HELP ME TO BE A BETTER PERSON!
ANDY, LOUIE
WHERE'S THE GUN?
WHY?
JUST CURIOUS.
IT'S HIDDEN.
WHERE?
NOWHERE.
YOU NEED TO GET IT OUT AGAIN.
WHY? I THOUGHT YOU WERE ALL OPPOSED TO IT.
THERE'S SOME UNFINISHED BUSINESS.
WHAT? STOOB?
I'VE GOT A PLAN.
NAH, THAT'S OKAY.
33.

THE LAST STRAW

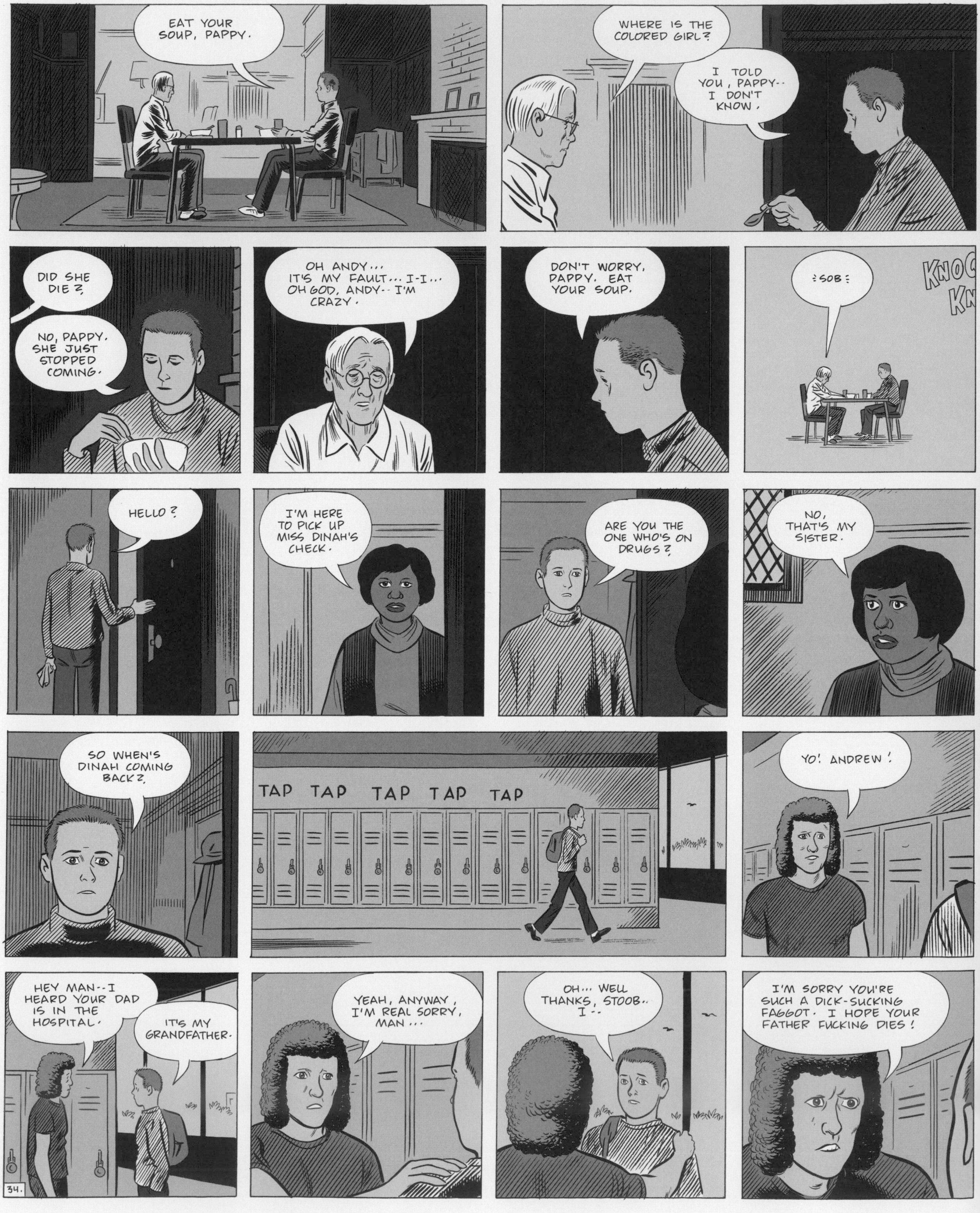

EAT YOUR SOUP, PAPPY.
WHERE IS THE COLORED GIRL?
I TOLD YOU, PAPPY-- I DON'T KNOW.
DID SHE DIE?
NO, PAPPY. SHE JUST STOPPED COMING.
OH ANDY... IT'S MY FAULT... I-I... OH GOD, ANDY-- I'M CRAZY.
DON'T WORRY, PAPPY. EAT YOUR SOUP.
SOB
KNOC
KN
HELLO?
I'M HERE TO PICK UP MISS DINAH'S CHECK.
ARE YOU THE ONE WHO'S ON DRUGS?
NO, THAT'S MY SISTER.
SO WHEN'S DINAH COMING BACK?
TAP TAP TAP TAP TAP
YO! ANDREW!
HEY MAN--I HEARD YOUR DAD IS IN THE HOSPITAL.
IT'S MY GRANDFATHER.
YEAH, ANYWAY, I'M REAL SORRY, MAN...
OH... WELL THANKS, STOOB.. I--
I'M SORRY YOU'RE SUCH A DICK-SUCKING FAGGOT. I HOPE YOUR FATHER FUCKING DIES!

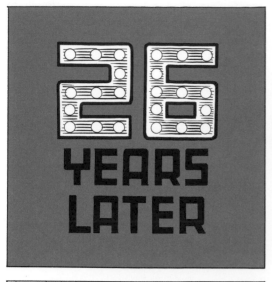

26 YEARS LATER

SO I WAS GOING TO TELL YOU ABOUT ALL THE TIMES I'VE FALLEN OFF THE WAGON...

I WAS GOOD FOR MANY YEARS. DIDN'T TOUCH TOBACCO AT ALL. IF SOMEONE GAVE ME GRIEF, I JUST STOOD THERE AND TOOK IT LIKE A MAN.

SO ONE DAY, THERE I WAS -- THIS IS AROUND THE TIME OF MY FIRST DIVORCE -- I'M IN THIS POLACK BAR ON THE WEST SIDE AND SOME DRUNK IS GIVING THE BARTENDER A HARD TIME WHILE HE AND HIS BUDDIES ARE TRYING TO WATCH A GAME.

NOTHING BIG, JUST BUGGING HIM, TRYING TO MAKE CONVERSATION.

LOOK, DUDE, I'M BUSY. WHY DON'T YOU GO SOMEWHERE ELSE?

I DON'T HAVE NOWHERE TO GO... LOOK, I'M NOT TRYING TO --. I JUST -- LOOK, I'M SORRY, MAN -- MY GRANDMOTHER DIED TODAY, Y'KNOW?

I DON'T GIVE A SHIT. WHO CARES? I'M TRYING TO WATCH THIS.

SO I SAY TO THE GUY NEXT TO ME, "HEY, HAVE YOU GOT A CIGARETTE?" I DIDN'T SMOKE IT RIGHT AWAY, THOUGH; I JUST WENT OUTSIDE AND WAITED.

BY THE TIME THE BARTENDER CLOSED UP I WAS STARTING TO FEEL A LITTLE SICK. IT HAD BEEN A LONG TIME.

STILL, I WAS ABLE TO DO SOME DAMAGE, AND I'LL BE DAMNED IF IT DIDN'T FEEL PRETTY GOOD.

A COUPLE WEEKS LATER I HAD ANOTHER SITUATION, AND ANOTHER A FEW WEEKS AFTER THAT. THERE'S ALWAYS SOME PRICK WHO NEEDS A LESSON. I NEVER LET IT GET OUT OF HAND, THOUGH, AND I NEVER EVEN THOUGHT ABOUT THE DEATH RAY.

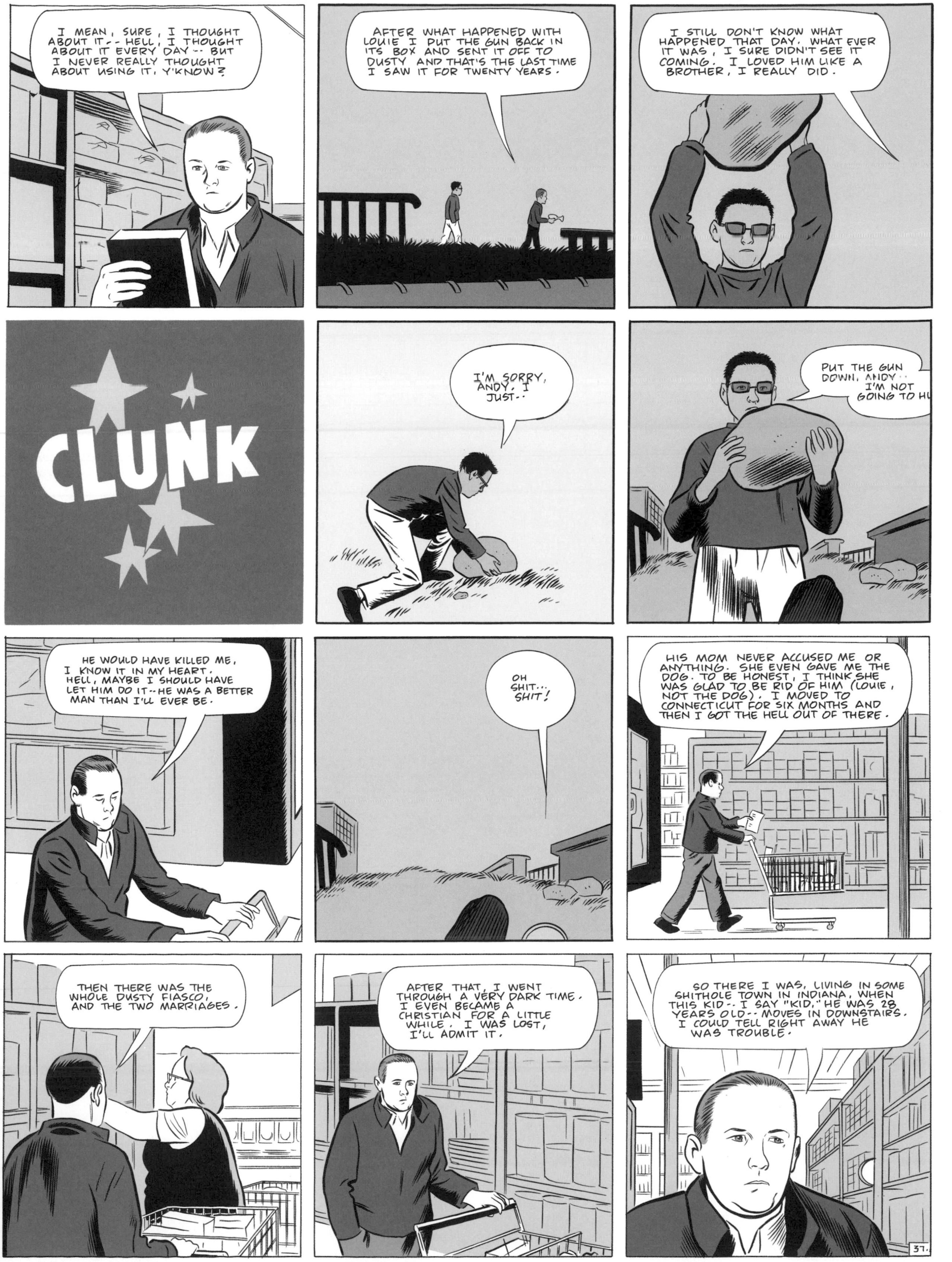
I MEAN, SURE, I THOUGHT ABOUT IT -- HELL, I THOUGHT ABOUT IT EVERY DAY -- BUT I NEVER REALLY THOUGHT ABOUT USING IT, Y'KNOW?
AFTER WHAT HAPPENED WITH LOUIE I PUT THE GUN BACK IN ITS BOX AND SENT IT OFF TO DUSTY AND THAT'S THE LAST TIME I SAW IT FOR TWENTY YEARS.
I STILL DON'T KNOW WHAT HAPPENED THAT DAY. WHAT EVER IT WAS, I SURE DIDN'T SEE IT COMING. I LOVED HIM LIKE A BROTHER, I REALLY DID.
CLUNK
I'M SORRY, ANDY, I JUST--
PUT THE GUN DOWN, ANDY-- I'M NOT GOING TO H
HE WOULD HAVE KILLED ME, I KNOW IT IN MY HEART. HELL, MAYBE I SHOULD HAVE LET HIM DO IT--HE WAS A BETTER MAN THAN I'LL EVER BE.
OH SHIT... SHIT!
HIS MOM NEVER ACCUSED ME OR ANYTHING. SHE EVEN GAVE ME THE DOG. TO BE HONEST, I THINK SHE WAS GLAD TO BE RID OF HIM (LOUIE, NOT THE DOG). I MOVED TO CONNECTICUT FOR SIX MONTHS AND THEN I GOT THE HELL OUT OF THERE.
THEN THERE WAS THE WHOLE DUSTY FIASCO, AND THE TWO MARRIAGES.
AFTER THAT, I WENT THROUGH A VERY DARK TIME. I EVEN BECAME A CHRISTIAN FOR A LITTLE WHILE. I WAS LOST, I'LL ADMIT IT.
SO THERE I WAS, LIVING IN SOME SHITHOLE TOWN IN INDIANA, WHEN THIS KID-- I SAY "KID," HE WAS 28 YEARS OLD-- MOVES IN DOWNSTAIRS. I COULD TELL RIGHT AWAY HE WAS TROUBLE.
37.

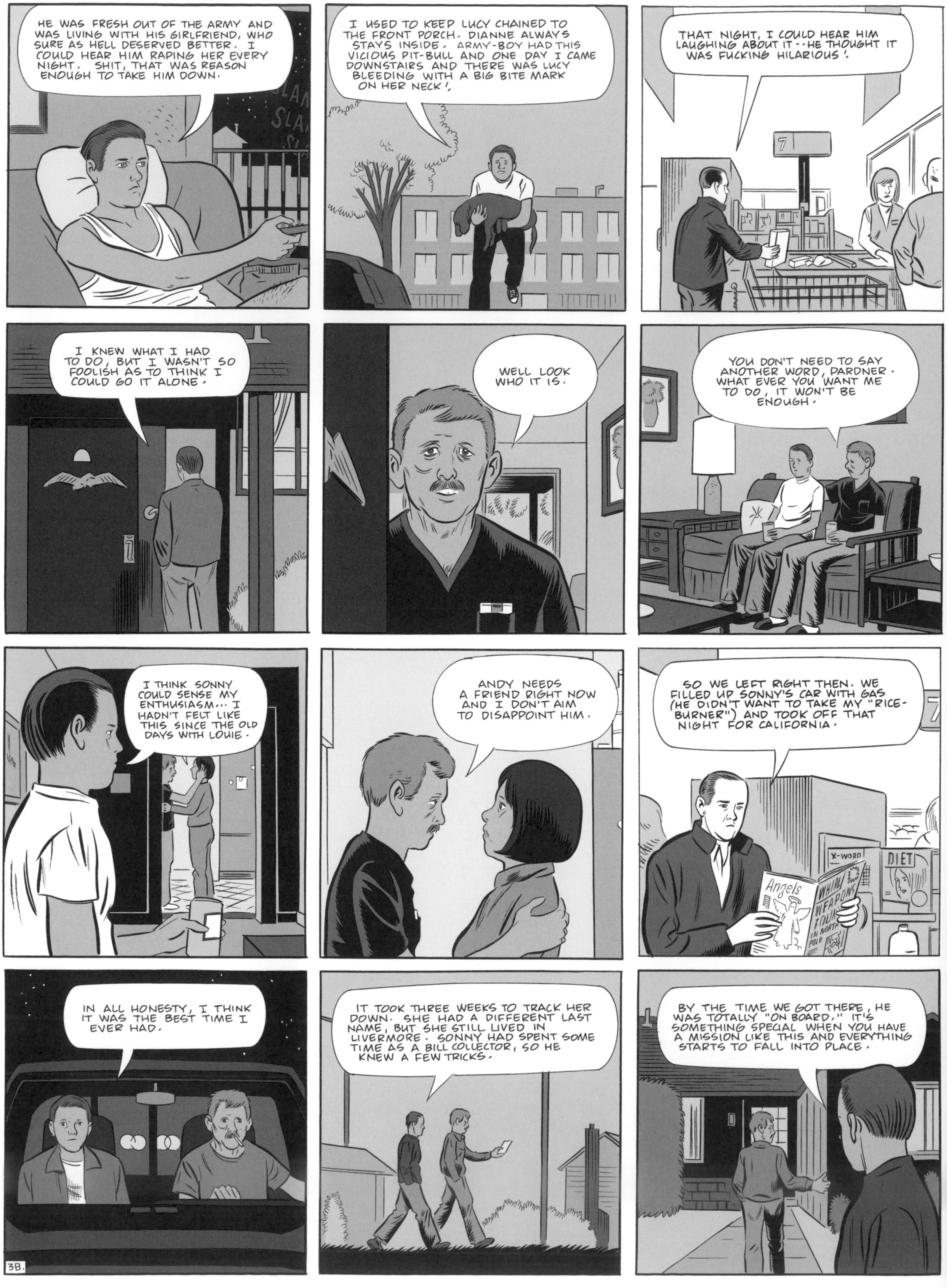
HE WAS FRESH OUT OF THE ARMY AND WAS LIVING WITH HIS GIRLFRIEND, WHO SURE AS HELL DESERVED BETTER. I COULD HEAR HIM RAPING HER EVERY NIGHT. SHIT, THAT WAS REASON ENOUGH TO TAKE HIM DOWN.
I USED TO KEEP LUCY CHAINED TO THE FRONT PORCH. DIANNE ALWAYS STAYS INSIDE. ARMY-BOY HAD THIS VICIOUS PIT-BULL AND ONE DAY I CAME DOWNSTAIRS AND THERE WAS LUCY BLEEDING WITH A BIG BITE MARK ON HER NECK!
THAT NIGHT, I COULD HEAR HIM LAUGHING ABOUT IT -- HE THOUGHT IT WAS FUCKING HILARIOUS!
7
I KNEW WHAT I HAD TO DO, BUT I WASN'T SO FOOLISH AS TO THINK I COULD GO IT ALONE.
WELL LOOK WHO IT IS.
YOU DON'T NEED TO SAY ANOTHER WORD, PARDNER. WHAT EVER YOU WANT ME TO DO, IT WON'T BE ENOUGH.
I THINK SONNY COULD SENSE MY ENTHUSIASM... I HADN'T FELT LIKE THIS SINCE THE OLD DAYS WITH LOUIE.
ANDY NEEDS A FRIEND RIGHT NOW AND I DON'T AIM TO DISAPPOINT HIM.
SO WE LEFT RIGHT THEN. WE FILLED UP SONNY'S CAR WITH GAS (HE DIDN'T WANT TO TAKE MY "RICE-BURNER") AND TOOK OFF THAT NIGHT FOR CALIFORNIA.
7
X-WORD
DIET
Angels
WEAPONS
IN NORTH POLE
IN ALL HONESTY, I THINK IT WAS THE BEST TIME I EVER HAD.
IT TOOK THREE WEEKS TO TRACK HER DOWN. SHE HAD A DIFFERENT LAST NAME, BUT SHE STILL LIVED IN LIVERMORE. SONNY HAD SPENT SOME TIME AS A BILL COLLECTOR, SO HE KNEW A FEW TRICKS.
BY THE TIME WE GOT THERE, HE WAS TOTALLY "ON BOARD." IT'S SOMETHING SPECIAL WHEN YOU HAVE A MISSION LIKE THIS AND EVERYTHING STARTS TO FALL INTO PLACE.

I MADE SONNY DO ALL THE WORK ONCE WE GOT THERE. I DIDN'T THINK IT WAS A GREAT IDEA TO SHOW MY FACE. BESIDES, HE HAS SUCH A GREAT WAY WITH PEOPLE.

SHE DIDN'T LOOK SO GOOD, I HAVE TO SAY, BUT IF I SQUINTED MY EYES I COULD SEE THE WAY SHE USED TO BE. I HADN'T STOPPED LOVING HER... AND STILL HAVEN'T TO THIS DAY, COME TO THINK OF IT.

BUT THAT'S NEITHER HERE NOR THERE. WE WERE ON A MISSION, AND THIS WAS JUST ONE STOP ALONG THE WAY.

SORRY, BUDDY -- SHE DOESN'T HAVE IT.

STILL, I THINK IT WAS A POSITIVE EXPERIENCE TO SEE HER AGAIN. ANYTHING THAT HELPS YOU TO UNDERSTAND YOUR OWN FEELINGS A BIT IS A PLUS IN MY BOOK.

THAT'S OKAY, BUDDY. LET IT OUT.

IT TOOK US ANOTHER TWO WEEKS TO TRACK DOWN THE GUN, AND THAT'S ONLY BECAUSE WE CAUGHT A LUCKY BREAK.

EVEN AFTER TWENTY YEARS I WAS ABLE TO DO A PRETTY GOOD DRAWING. I'M NOTHING IF NOT CLEAR-HEADED.

I THINK I SEEN THIS IN A SHOP OVER TO BAKERSFIELD.

WE GOT THERE JUST IN TIME -- HE WAS JUST ABOUT TO SELL IT ON THE COMPUTER. I HAD TO PAY FOUR HUNDRED DOLLARS FOR MY OWN DAMN GUN!

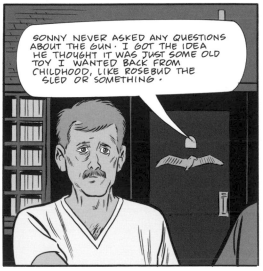

SONNY NEVER ASKED ANY QUESTIONS ABOUT THE GUN. I GOT THE IDEA HE THOUGHT IT WAS JUST SOME OLD TOY I WANTED BACK FROM CHILDHOOD, LIKE ROSEBUD THE SLED OR SOMETHING.

ANYWAY, I WENT BACK HOME AND TOOK CARE OF MY BUSINESS. EVERYONE WAS RELIEVED AND I FELT GOOD ABOUT IT. TWO MONTHS LATER I GOT THE HELL OUT OF INDIANA AND MOVED BACK TO THE OLD NEIGHBORHOOD.

I GUESS I ALWAYS KNEW I'D WIND UP BACK HERE EVENTUALLY. HELL, WHERE ELSE AM I GOING TO GO?

WHEN I WAS YOUNGER I USED TO DREAM ABOUT FINDING THE PERFECT PLACE TO LIVE... THE KIND OF PLACE WHERE PEOPLE TREAT EACH OTHER RIGHT, Y'KNOW? WELL GUESS WHAT? I NEVER FOUND IT.

EXCUSE ME?

39

THE UNITED STATES OF ANDY

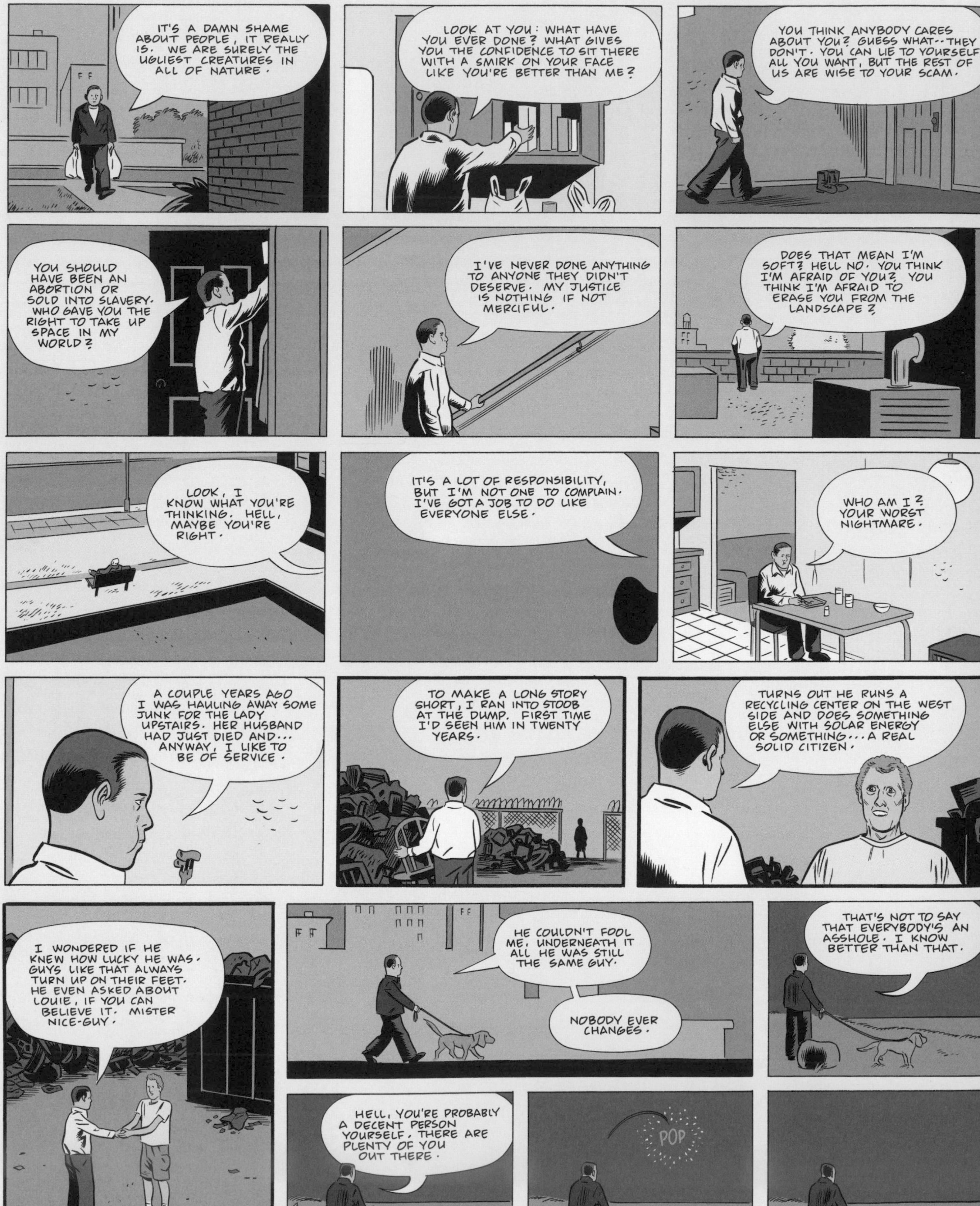
IT'S A DAMN SHAME ABOUT PEOPLE, IT REALLY IS. WE ARE SURELY THE UGLIEST CREATURES IN ALL OF NATURE.
LOOK AT YOU: WHAT HAVE YOU EVER DONE? WHAT GIVES YOU THE CONFIDENCE TO SIT THERE WITH A SMIRK ON YOUR FACE LIKE YOU'RE BETTER THAN ME?
YOU THINK ANYBODY CARES ABOUT YOU? GUESS WHAT-- THEY DON'T. YOU CAN LIE TO YOURSELF ALL YOU WANT, BUT THE REST OF US ARE WISE TO YOUR SCAM.
YOU SHOULD HAVE BEEN AN ABORTION OR SOLD INTO SLAVERY. WHO GAVE YOU THE RIGHT TO TAKE UP SPACE IN MY WORLD?
I'VE NEVER DONE ANYTHING TO ANYONE THEY DIDN'T DESERVE. MY JUSTICE IS NOTHING IF NOT MERCIFUL.
DOES THAT MEAN I'M SOFT? HELL NO. YOU THINK I'M AFRAID OF YOU? YOU THINK I'M AFRAID TO ERASE YOU FROM THE LANDSCAPE?
LOOK, I KNOW WHAT YOU'RE THINKING. HELL, MAYBE YOU'RE RIGHT.
IT'S A LOT OF RESPONSIBILITY, BUT I'M NOT ONE TO COMPLAIN. I'VE GOT A JOB TO DO LIKE EVERYONE ELSE.
WHO AM I? YOUR WORST NIGHTMARE.
A COUPLE YEARS AGO I WAS HAULING AWAY SOME JUNK FOR THE LADY UPSTAIRS. HER HUSBAND HAD JUST DIED AND... ANYWAY, I LIKE TO BE OF SERVICE.
TO MAKE A LONG STORY SHORT, I RAN INTO STOOB AT THE DUMP. FIRST TIME I'D SEEN HIM IN TWENTY YEARS.
TURNS OUT HE RUNS A RECYCLING CENTER ON THE WEST SIDE AND DOES SOMETHING ELSE WITH SOLAR ENERGY OR SOMETHING... A REAL SOLID CITIZEN.
I WONDERED IF HE KNEW HOW LUCKY HE WAS. GUYS LIKE THAT ALWAYS TURN UP ON THEIR FEET. HE EVEN ASKED ABOUT LOUIE, IF YOU CAN BELIEVE IT. MISTER NICE-GUY.
HE COULDN'T FOOL ME. UNDERNEATH IT ALL HE WAS STILL THE SAME GUY.
NOBODY EVER CHANGES.
THAT'S NOT TO SAY THAT EVERYBODY'S AN ASSHOLE. I KNOW BETTER THAN THAT.
HELL, YOU'RE PROBABLY A DECENT PERSON YOURSELF. THERE ARE PLENTY OF YOU OUT THERE.
POP

WHY DID ANDY DESTROY YOU?

I SOLD SOME GRASS TO HIS MAID'S DAUGHTER.

I FUCKED HIS WIFE.

I FUCKED HIS OTHER WIFE.

IT WAS MY OWN FAULT, REALLY. I'M SORRY, ANDY.

WHAT DO YOU THINK OF ANDY (AGAIN)?

SAY WHAT YOU WILL ABOUT ANDY, HE'S NUMBER ONE IN MY BOOK.

PLEASE, NO ANDY QUESTIONS.

MAY GOD FIND A WAY INTO HIS HEART.

OH ANDY...

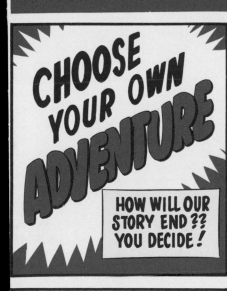

CHOOSE YOUR OWN ADVENTURE

HOW WILL OUR STORY END?? YOU DECIDE!

A. ANDY ZAPS EVERYONE IN THE WORLD UNTIL HE'S THE ONLY ONE LEFT.

B. HE TURNS THE GUN ON HIMSELF AND THE WORLD GOES ON WITHOUT HIM.

C. HE CONTINUES TO LIVE MUCH AS HE HAS FOR THE PAST TWENTY-FIVE YEARS. AFTER DIANNE DIES HE GETS A FOX TERRIER NAMED MICKEY, AND AFTER THAT, A COLLIE. HE WRONG-HEADEDLY PURSUES A DIVORCEE ON THE THIRD FLOOR AND SHORTLY THEREAFTER DATES A WOMAN IN HER SIXTIES FOR SEVERAL YEARS. HE RETIRES FROM HIS JOB AT THE LIBRARY WITH THE INTENTION OF MOVING TO NORTHERN CALIFORNIA BUT FINDS IT TOO EXPENSIVE. HE REMOVES FROM EXISTENCE A PRIEST, A MAN WHO SPITS ON PIGEONS, AND THE EX HUSBAND OF THE DIVORCEE ON THE THIRD FLOOR. HE BURIES THE DEATH RAY IN A SHALLOW HOLE IN THE INDIANA DUNES. HE BURNS HIS DAD'S PAPERS AND SCATTERS THE ASHES IN THE LAKE. AT SOME POINT HE DIES, PROBABLY OF LUNG CANCER.

PAFFF

FOR YOU, MR. AND MRS. DECENT CITIZEN, I'LL DO ANYTHING. JUST SAY THE WORD.

BOOM!

BAM! BADAM BA

YOU'VE GOT A FRIEND IN OLD ANDY.

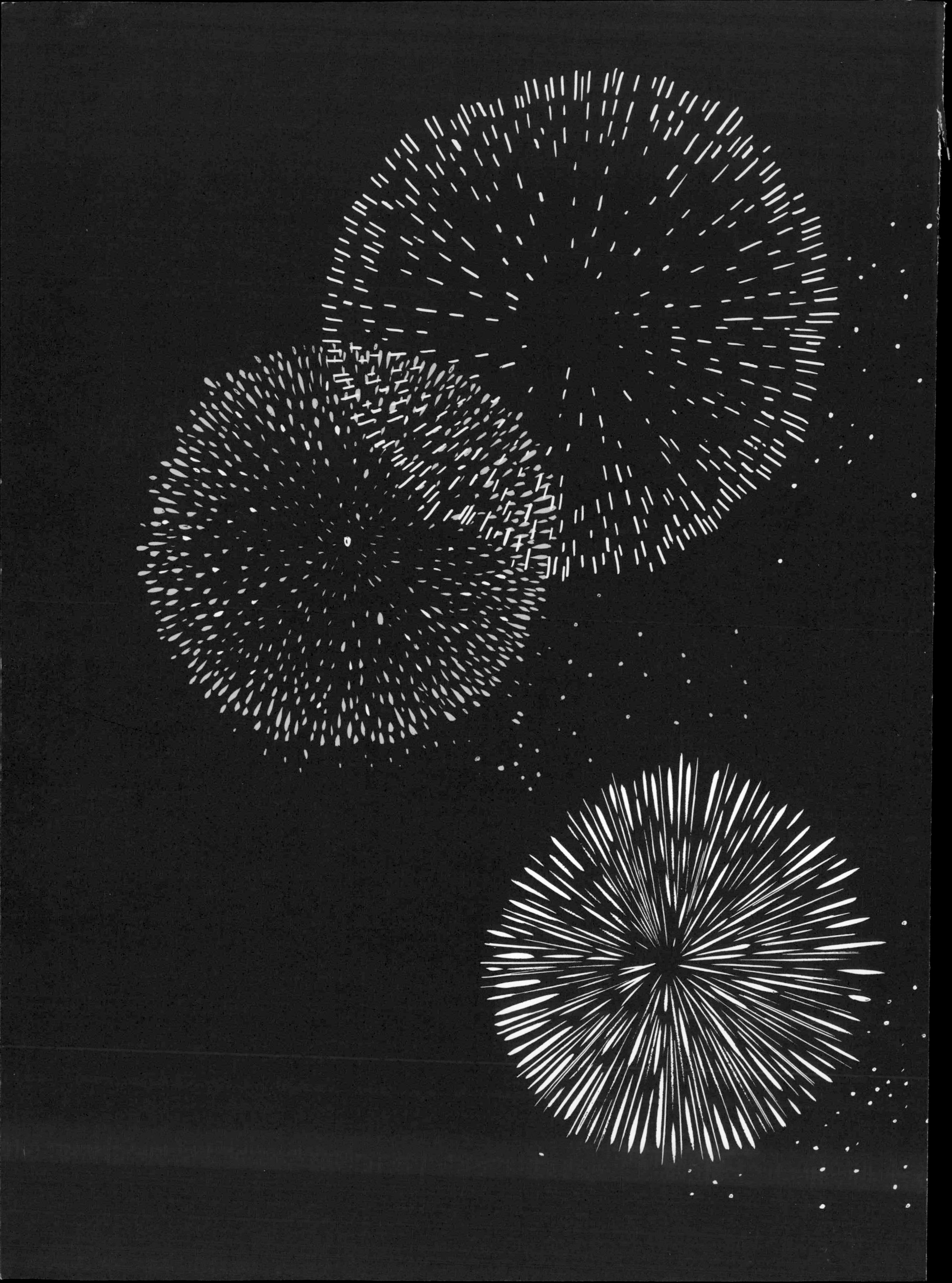

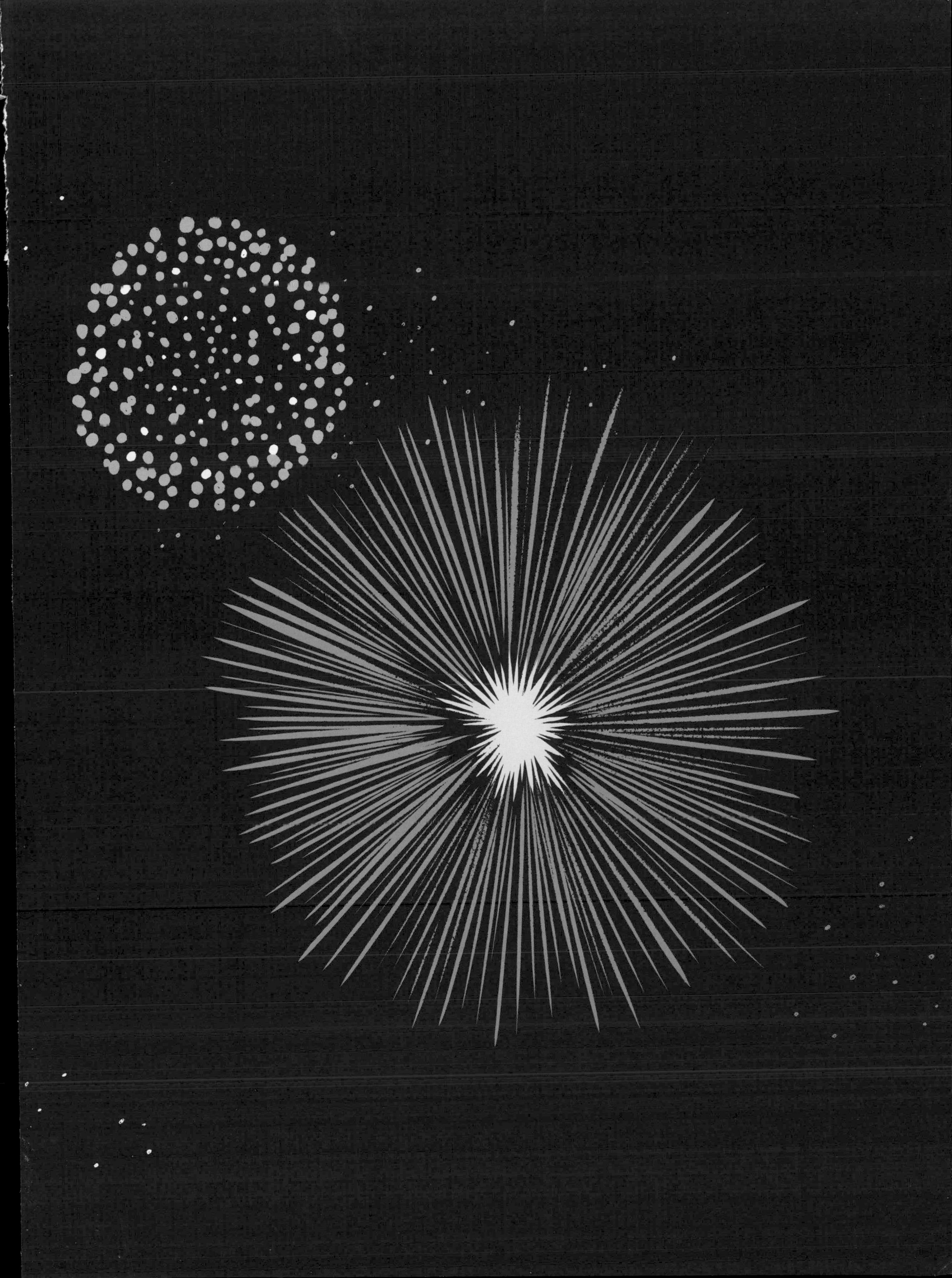

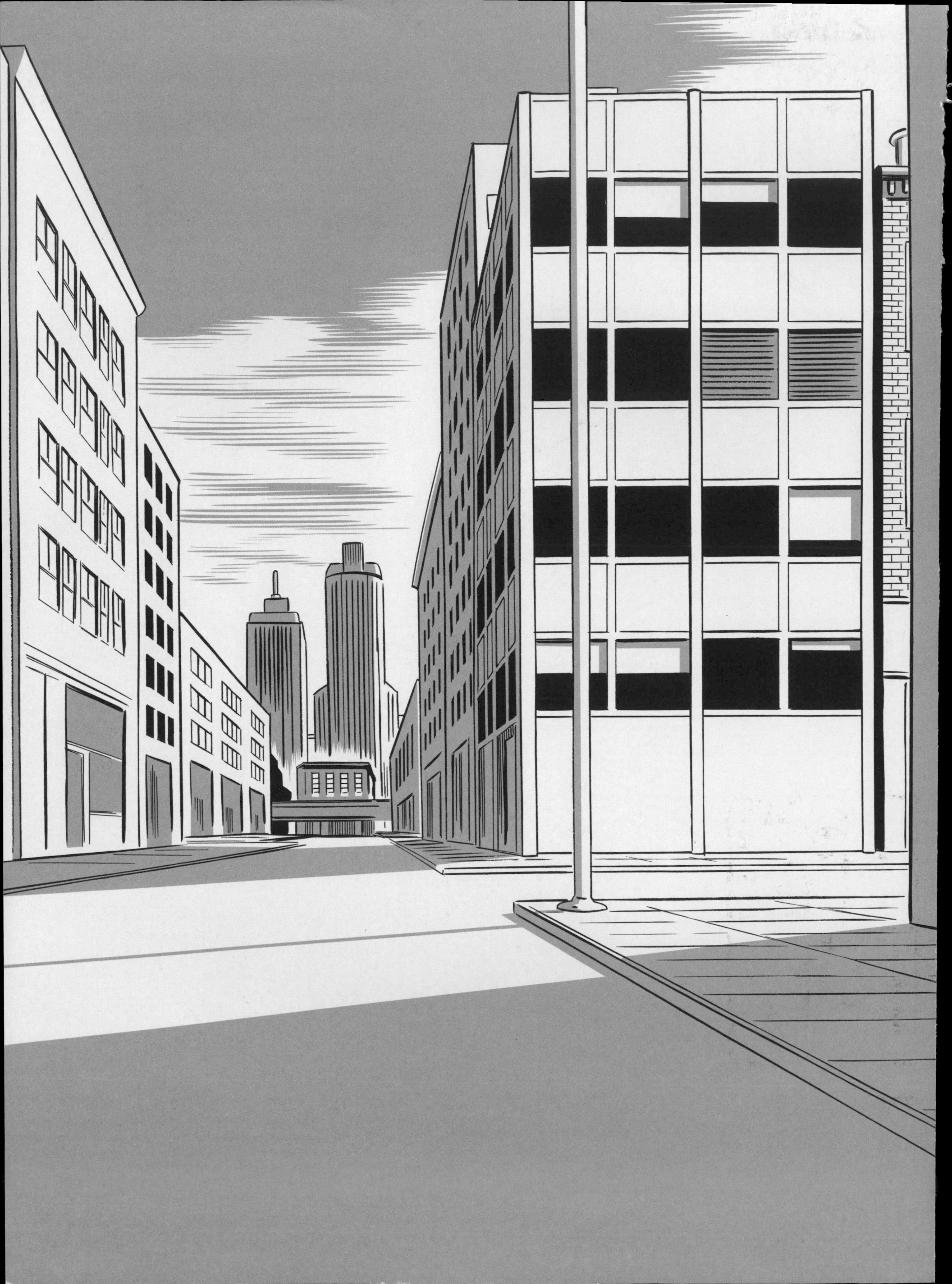